Europe
1815-1870

Edited by

Peter Catterall

and

Richard Vinen

Heinemann

HISTORY BRIEFINGS

Heinemann Educational
a division of Heinemann Publishers (Oxford) Ltd.
Halley Court, Jordan Hill, Oxford OX2 8EJ

OXFORD   LONDON   EDINBURGH
MELBOURNE   MADRID   ATHENS
BOLOGNA   PARIS   SYDNEY
AUCKLAND   SINGAPORE   TOKYO
IBADAN   NAIROBI   HARARE
GABORONE   PORTSMOUTH NH (USA)

First published 1994

British Library Cataloguing in Publication Data

A catalogue record for this book is available from the British Library

ISBN 0 435 31003 8

98 97 96 95
10 9 8 7 6 5 4 3 2

Typeset by CentraCet Ltd, Cambridge

Printed and bound in Great Britain by Clay Ltd, St Ives plc.

Front cover: *Liberty leading the People* by Eugène Delacroix
(Bridgeman Art Library/The Louvre, Paris)

Acknowledgements

Heinemann and the ICBH wish to thank all the contributors who
have given permission for their work to be published in this book.

Thanks are also due to Philip Allan (Publishers) Ltd for permission
to print articles which originally appeared in the *Modern History
Review*.

Contents

Part I: Revolution and Reaction

Introduction   5
Richard Vinen

The Legacy of the French Revolution   11
William Doyle

Castlereagh's Foreign Policy   22
John Derry

France 1814–48: Monarchy and its Enemies   34
Pamela Pilbeam

Alexander I of Russia: Reformer or Reactionary?   42
David Saunders

Europe in Revolt: The 1848 Revolutions   50
William Fortescue

The Serfs' Perspective on Emancipation   59
David Moon

**Part II: Nationalism and the Breakup of the
Vienna Settlement**

Introduction   67
Richard Vinen

The Greek War of Independence   70
Richard Clogg

The Risorgimento's Failure: Italian Unification and After   78
Jonathan Morris

The Unification of Germany   87
Michael John

The Crimean War 1854–56: An Historical Illusion?   99
Andrew Lambert

Idealist or Opportunist: Reassessing Napoleon III   109
James McMillan

Examiner's Report   117
Patrick Condren

PART I
Revolution and Reaction

Modern European history is overshadowed by the legacy of two revolutions. The first of these is the political revolution that began in France in 1789, the second was the industrial revolution that began in England in the late eighteenth century. The impact of the first of these revolutions is to be seen in many of the developments described below by William Doyle. The rituals and rhetoric of the French Revolution were to be found in all sorts of events over the next two hundred years. The *Marseillaise* was to be sung by revolutionaries like Lenin, and by conservatives such as Marshal Pétain. It is, however, possible to overestimate the direct political legacy of the Revolution. Napoleon had restored orderly government and authority to France by the early nineteenth century. Aristocrats were filling government jobs again long before the restoration of the Bourbon monarchy in 1814–15. Sometimes there were unexpected continuities across the whole period. Quick footed politicians like Fouché and Talleyrand managed to pop up under widely differing regimes. Louix XVIII, who returned to rule France after the revolution, even sat on the same throne that had been used by Napoleon.

The years after 1789 can be seen as a gradual process of stabilisation in which conflict about constitutional arrangements among the ruling classes was replaced by unity in defence of social privileges. In the 1820s, liberals, like Benjamin Constant, stressed that they did not support a return to revolutionary ideas. The subsequent failure of the various monarchies in nineteenth century France had more to do with personal failings, economic crisis and military defeat than with memories of 1789. It is also possible to overestimate the impact of the French Revolution outside France. Lord Salisbury was so haunted by fear of the French Revolution that he had nightmares about Jacobins attempting to storm his own library at Hatfield House. However, Salisbury was a neurotic intellectual who was uncharacteristic of his class. Bismarck, who had fought against real revolutionaries in 1848, took a tougher view: he showed himself willing to ally with revolutionaries when it suited his purpose, and he even wrote that he would have served a republic as readily as a monarch if he had happened to be born under such a regime. The most important legacies of the French Revolution were in the field of economics and class relations rather than ideology, and the first of these concerned the structure of the family itself.

More than anything the French Revolution was a revolt against primogeniture: the system by which eldest sons inherited the titles and properties of their fathers. Such a system produced deep bitterness among younger sons and in spite of its emphasis on 'fraternité' the Revolution saw some murderous displays of sibling rivalry. The Duke of Orleans voted for the death of his own brother, Louis XVI. This stimulated a split between 'orleanists' and 'legitimists' which some historians have associated with a broader class hostility between liberal capitalism and Catholic aristocratic government. Many of the aristocrats who returned to France and accepted posts under Napoleon were younger sons, who were seeking to oust their elder brothers. The Comte de Mirabeau, a revolutionary who quarrelled violently with his elder brother, arranged for primogeniture to be abolished altogether. This was to have important consequences for the French peasantry. It ensured that the characteristic structure of French agriculture would be the small peasant farm that sprang from equal division among heirs. It also ensured that the French population would remain static at around forty million people for the whole period of the Third Republic (between 1870 and 1940): population increase at this stage would have meant that farms became divided into unfeasibly small units.

The other great social legacy of the French Revolution concerned war. The Revolution was followed by wars against the powers who sought to help restore the monarchy; these were followed by Napoleon's military adventures. The Revolutionary Wars were novel in being fought by 'citizens' armies' made up of the 'nation in arms' who were summoned to defend their country by the *levée en masse*. The idea of the 'nation in arms' was to have important consequences. The novelist, Céline, complained that the notion that people had a duty to die for their country without financial reward was an invention of the French Revolution. Throughout Europe citizens' militias became associated with the defence of the political system. Eventually the citizens' army gave birth to the idea of universal military service that was to have such an impact on the lives of most inhabitants of continental Europe. The link between military service and citizenship was to remain: it was no accident that the only major country without universal male military service in 1914 (Great Britain) was also the only country without universal male suffrage.

The soldiers of the army with which Napoleon had conquered much of Europe were disbanded in 1815 and scattered across France. They were bitter men, epitomized by Charles Bovary's father in Flaubert's *Madame Bovary*, and were to spend much of the rest of their lives recalling their past glories and hence contributing to the myths that began to surround Napoleon – myths that the

Emperor cultivated assiduously during his exile on St Helena between 1815 and 1821. The Revolutionary Wars also left a less direct legacy. During these wars, state employment had expanded in every European country – the raising of taxation, the conscription of soldiers and the transport of supplies all required an administrative apparatus. In France the number of customs officers alone increased from 12,000 to 35,000.

By the end of the wars, many young men had grown up expecting that the state would provide them with employment. The numbers of such men were swelled by several things. Firstly, universities on the continent were relatively cheap and democratic – it was easy to acquire an education. In Lombardy-Venetia, the number of university students doubled in the twenty years after 1815. In Britain, by contrast, universities were expensive and exclusive. Most graduates were either wealthy enough to support themselves or were assured of posts in the Church (which had independent resources to subsidize such employment). Secondly, there was a slight increase in the birth rate after 1815. In France birth rates peaked in 1826, and it was no accident that these young men were to reach maturity in the revolutionary year of 1848. Thirdly, the myth of the career open to talents spread through much of Europe in the aftermath of the French Revolution. This myth was exacerbated by the success of Napoleon (the ultimate local boy made good) who made himself the spokesman of youthful ambition when he said that a successful army should contain 'young generals and old capitans'.

Unfortunately, there were few jobs for educated young men who flocked to cities in search of fame and fortune during the early nineteenth century. This was partly because of a cut in public spending after the Napoleonic Wars. The Austrian government insisted that state officials should serve an unpaid 'pupilship', which might last for up to twelve years. It was also partly because a generation of men had been appointed to posts at a young age during the wars. These men now held on to their jobs while they aged and blocked all possibility of promotion for their juniors.

In France 15% of departmental prefects had been aged over 50 in 1818; by 1830 this figure had reached 55%. Indeed France institutionalised the hegemony of age over youth: men could not be elected to office before the age of forty. A Swiss writer described France as a 'gerontocracy' which was ruled by 'seven or eight thousand gouty eligibles.' Similiar problems beset other countries where the 'excess of educated men' (Leonore O'Boyle) were unable to find employment. In Prussia, in 1835, it was estimated that there were 262 candidates for every 100 vacancies in the Church, and 250 candidates for every judicial vacancy. Educated and unemployed men were obliged to make do with insecure and insubstantial jobs as tutors or journalists. Not surprisingly their dissatisfaction with the regime often made them prone to radical ideas, and it was not surprising to find unemployed lawyers and journalists behind many of the revolutionary and nationalist outbreaks in Europe during the mid-nineteenth century. The Italian democractic leader, Constabile Carducci, was typical of the breed. He had qualified as a lawyer, but subsequently he was obliged to earn his living as an innkeeper and a carrier.

The French Revolution had produced a gulf between Britain and continental Europe. The gulf was widened by the impact of the Industrial Revolution. Between 1815 and 1850, the British economy grew by an average of 3.5% per annum, while that of France only grew at around 2.5% per annum. In 1851 over half of the British population, compared to 25% of that of Germany and France, lived in towns; only 25% of the British workforce, compared to 50% of that of Belgium, worked in agriculture. The full extent of Britain's success was not always apparent to contemporaries (John Stuart Mill nervously calculated that British coal reserves would soon run out), but, in retrospect, it is clear that Britain was a world superpower at a time when continental European governments were still hard-pressed to maintain their influence over their own nations. The roots of British success lay partly in natural resources. Coal was a crucial component of early industrialisation, and it was a commodity that Britain possessed in abundance. By contrast parts of Europe that lacked coal such as Holland, especially after her separation from Belgium in 1839, and the West of France, after it lost access to imports from Britain, stagnated. Good transport was another key. Britain was relatively small and it possessed good access to the sea, which was often the only cheap means of transporting goods in bulk. Every other European economy remained fragmented. In Holland inland wages were half those in coastal regions and coal was twice as expensive inland as in coastal regions.

Certain social differences also accounted for the divergence between Britain and the Continent. In Britain, aristocrats were involved in industrial investment on a scale far larger than in continental Europe and the peasantry had been replaced by large scale 'agrarian capitalism'. The social influence of the French Revolution was also intimately tied up with the ways in which the Industrial Revolution spread, or failed to spread, through continental Europe. For much of society it might be argued that political or economic revolution represented alternative paths to modernity. On the Continent, ambitious young men looked to politics and state employment; in England such young men, often excluded by religion or poverty from higher education and public life, were forced to make their careers in industry. In France the seizure and sale of land that belonged to the Church or to anti-revolutionary aristocrats also had a socially regressive effect. Far from bringing about the replacement of 'backward' aristocrats by a progressive 'bourgeoisie', such sales encouraged merchants to invest in the purchase of lands rather than in industry. Indeed, some groups, like the Say family of western France, moved out of trade entirely as they bought up land. Eventually, the obsession with land ownership as the measure of social success spread through French society and came to dominate the peasantry. This obsession helps to explain the predominantly rural and agricultural basis of France that lasts up to the present day. Shifts in French agriculture were exacerbated by the British blockade that began in 1806. This blockade destroyed the trade of Atlantic ports; 121 American ships came into Bordeaux in 1807, the following year this figure had dropped to 6. The blockade encouraged the 'pasturalization' of the West of France. It had political consequences. It was no accident that the West produced some of the most violent reactions against the French Revolution, and that the underdeveloped West soon came to be seen as a centre of social and political conservatism. It also had economic consequences for the whole of Europe. The economic centre of gravity shifted away from the Atlantic trade towards that based on the Rhine. Strasbourg prospered while Bordeaux declined.

The simple cost of fighting the Revolutionary Wars also drained resources from continental Europe that might otherwise have been invested in industry. Between 1812 and 1814, the British had maintained about 250,000 men in arms, the French had maintained 600,000 and the Russians 500,000. Britain was able to remain relatively insulated from European wars because of its island status and the strength of its fleet (at the end of the Napoleonic wars, it had 214 ships compared with France's 80). British seapower laid the foundation for its trade and for its lucrative imperial adventures. It also ensured that Britain was able to protect itself at very little cost after 1815. At the height of its economic and imperial power, in the mid-nineteenth century, Britain spent a tiny proportion of its resources on its own defence. By contrast, other European powers were still obliged to maintain high spending on defence against their neighbours: in 1830, France had over 250,000 men in its armies, Russia had over 800,000 and Prussia had over 200,000.

Economic growth in Europe differed qualitatively as well as quantitatively from that of Britain. British capitalism had been based on relatively cheap technology and on simple informal finance, which was often raised by borrowing within families or by local attorneys. Continental industrialisation occurred later at a time when technology was more sophisticated and more expensive, and when newly founded industries had to survive the competition that was already provided by Britain. All this meant that higher levels of initial investment were needed. Joint stock banks, such as the Belgian Société Générale, sprang up to fill this need. The state also played a larger role in Europe than it had done in Britain. Sometimes this intervention was provoked by political pressures. In a bid to buy off rebellion, the Dutch government lent about 5,821,000 florins to their southern provinces between 1824 and 1830. If British industrialisation revolved around the *laissez-faire* that was defined by Adam Smith, continental industrialisation often revolved, consciously or not, around the 'National Economics' (defined in a book published by Friederich List in 1841). List emphasised the need for the state to protect young industries from competition with tariffs.

The nature of economic growth in continental Europe had political consequences as well as political causes. The extent to which the bourgeoisie in continental Europe remained dependent on the state – either as civil servants, would-be civil servants, or industrialists who needed tariffs – helps to account for the fact that liberalism was unsuccessful in countries like Germany. The fact that the continental economy remained so heavily dependent on agriculture helps to explain why bursts of discontent, such as those that occurred in the 1840s, could be provoked by harvest failures. Most importantly, the interplay between politics and economics in continental Europe was seen in the fate of groups like the peasantry and the artisans. These groups were often seen as economically redundant in the age of capitalist economy and factory production. In Britain the first group had more or less ceased to exist and the second had lost much of its independence. However, in continental Europe, governments feared the political consequences of allowing such groups to be eliminated. Metternich and Bismarck were ruthless men, but they could not have regarded the destruction of large social groups with the indifference that marked the British aristocracy's attitude to the Highland clearances, the enclosure of the common land, or the Irish potato famine. The spread of suffrage in the nineteenth century gave 'backward' groups ever more power. Furthermore, industrial modernisation which might have damaged such groups in economic terms increased their power in political terms. Governments became increasingly dependent on small and traditional producers to provide a political counter-weight to the growing power of the organised working class. This dependence was to dominate European politics until at least the mid-twentieth century.

William Doyle
The Legacy of the French Revolution

The French Revolution played a crucial part in shaping the political ideas, attitudes and conflicts of the nineteenth century.

Is the French Revolution over? That must seem like a rather silly question to ask about an event that took place, or at least began, two centuries ago. But the question is not as silly as it sounds. After all, only in 1989 we were invited by President Mitterand to celebrate the 200th anniversary of the fall of the Bastille, not just as a spectacular event in the past, but as a symbol of what was also proclaimed in France during that distant and turbulent summer, the Rights of Man. Amid assembled world leaders on 13 July 1989 an actress solemnly read out the Declaration of the Rights of Man and the Citizen; and shortly afterwards the atmosphere was poisoned by the intervention of Margaret Thatcher declaring that the Rights of Man were not a French invention at all, but were the work of the British, if not the ancient Greeks. She probably should not have said it. It was extremely rude to disparage somebody else's celebration in this way, especially when she was a guest – even if there were senses in which she was right. But what is interesting is that she thought it worth saying at all. It meant she *cared about* the French Revolution as indeed, from his own viewpoint, did President Mitterand. They both clearly thought that the revolution lay at the root of things that we still think important today, for good (in Mitterand's case) or ill (in Thatcher's). The French Revolution, in other words, remains a living issue: and in that sense at least it is certainly *not* over.

And what makes it a living issue? It is the fact that it marks the beginning of a whole range of attitudes, values, ideals, institutions and ways of doing things that have swept the world ever since and are very largely still with us. Perhaps the first point to be made about the legacy of the Revolution is that it is practically limitless. Try to imagine the modern world without it having taken place: it would be practically impossible. The world would not probably have been much different today if Queen Elizabeth, or Louis XIV, or Gladstone, or even Genghis Khan had never existed. To adapt the famous quip of Voltaire, if they hadn't existed, somebody would have invented them. It's a game worth playing with all sorts of historical characters and phenomena, a way of assessing what difference they actually made. But the only movements comparable in scope and long-term impact to the French Revolution, I would argue, are religious ones such as Christianity, Islam, or the Reformation, ones which have affected, or attempted to affect every aspect of peoples' lives.

The idea of revolution

Take for example the very idea of Revolution itself. Our modern conception of it goes back no further than 1789. Before that, revolution simply meant political change. The fall of a minister, a change of monarch, a change of policy, even – all these were indiscriminately called revolutions by people in the eighteenth-century. But what happened in France in and after 1789 changed all that. It *was* a revolution, of course, in the old sense, a spectacular political change. But the extent of that change, as it developed over subsequent years, was so great, and so far-reaching, that it soon became clear that this was an upheaval quite unlike any other that had happened before, and that if this was a revolution then the meaning of the word had to be changed. And so it was. Ever since then, we have always been careful to distinguish between mere change, and even simple *coups d'état*, and real, full-blooded revolution. And people were doing it right from the start. When the Americans, who had just thrown off British authority, talked in the 1790s of the American Revolution of the 1770s, the French were dismissive. What had happened in America, they said, was not revolutionary at all compared with what had happened in France. What had happened there was something altogether more profound and fundamental. And since that time, the French Revolution has been generally recognised as the classic example of one, the model against which all subsequent revolutions are judged.

But not only is it a model; it is a pattern. This is how revolutions *work*. That means that it has been endlessly studied, pored over, thought about, analysed both by political scientists seeking to explain how and why revolutions work, and by more practical people who want to know how to bring one about; or alternatively how to prevent one. Because what the French Revolution showed was that states could be overthrown by mass action, and whole new patterns of authority and society set up under a new order. This too was completely new. There had of course been mass revolts before, since the beginning of history, but they had hardly ever succeeded unless they were backed by more organised force; and over the century and a half or so preceding 1789 they were by and large even less successful than before, because most states now had standing armies of professional soldiers who always triumphed in the end. But the events of 1789 showed that they did not *need* to. The biggest army in Europe failed to prevent the fall of the Bastille. The state could be defied, and destroyed, and replaced. And this was both an inspiration, and a warning. Those who disliked the status quo they lived under, whatever it was, now knew that it might be vulnerable, or made so by doing the right things. And so a completely new character in human affairs was born: the revolutionary, the person who plans and works towards the overthrow of the existing order by violent action, in order to take over power and make radical changes. No such people existed before 1789, because there was no precedent, no pattern, to inspire them and guide them. After the French Revolution, there was. In fact, after that, precedents multiplied all the time, so that for much of the nineteenth and twentieth centuries revolution, or the threat of it, was, as Karl Marx put it, a spectre haunting Europe. French history upto the 1870s was a series of re-runs of the original revolution, whether we are talking about 1830, or 1848, or 1871. The 1790s were in everybody's mind, whether as a set of guidelines to follow or a catalogue of mistakes to avoid. And the French experience was much in the mind of all communist revolutionaries, from Marx to Lenin, as they plotted their own schemes for the violent overthrow of a bad old world in order to inaugurate a better way of running human affairs.

Events of the French Revolution upto 1793

1789

May	Meeting of the States General
June	Third Estate proclaims the National Assembly. The aim is to prepare a French Constitution.
July	Fall of the Bastille in Paris
Aug	Declaration of the Rights of Man

1790

New Constitution framed

1791

June	Flight of Louis XVI to Varennes
Oct	Louis XVI approves France's first Constitution. The monarch is now only a figure-head. Power is invested in the Legislative Assembly made up of 745 deputies elected by 50,000 voters. The Assembly meets for the first time on 1 October.

1792

June	Attack on the Tuileries Palace
July	Prussia declares war on France as foreign powers threaten to intervene in the affairs of Revolutionary France.
Aug	The monarchy is suspended
Sept	Danton organises the National Defence against foreign armies National Convention meets and abolishes the monarchy. France is now a republic.

1793

Jan	Execution of Louis XVI

Conservative responses

For them, then, an inspiration: but for governments, a warning and a threat. States are vulnerable; and in the right circumstances they can be overthrown. One of the first jobs of government, therefore, is to keep an eye on subversives, watch out for revolutionaries, and harass, persecute, imprison, and if necessary kill them. Secret policemen were *not* an invention of the French Revolution. Governments began to employ informers and eavesdroppers before the 1780s in various places. But *after* 1789 it became standard practice everywhere, because now you were looking not for random subversives but for systematic plotters aiming at wholesale revolution, and to get them you had to be equally systematic.

Since the French Revolution *all* states have had a secret police, whether you call it the KGB, the Gestapo, the Securitate, the FBI, or the Special Branch. But what the French Revolution also showed is that revolutions are mass movements. Secret police can keep tabs on professional agitators and revolutionaries, but they can't control whole disaffected populations. For that, you need either a much more comprehensive repressive apparatus, meaning above all an army designed more for internal than external use – what might be called the Metternich solution; or else you need to pursue policies or create conditions where the mass of the people are not deeply discontented. In other words you reform to preserve, reform to avoid revolution. This is what you might call the English Whig solution. But either way you build an outlook around the possibility of revolution and violent overthrow; and as much as radicalism, therefore, the French Revolution created conservatism as a coherent, thought-out political stance. Before 1789 in general, the status quo did not need to be justified or defended. It was simply there; and apart from tinkering around with surface details it could not really be changed or altered in any fundamental way. Political changes might be possible, but scarcely social ones. But the revolution showed that comprehensive and far-reaching political *and* social changes were possible; that society, indeed, could be turned upside down, its traditional rulers persecuted and executed in droves, the church destroyed, and the policies of a state dictated to by bloodthirsty and levelling mobs. Not only did this example scare established orders everywhere. It forced them into trying to *justify* themselves, to defend the way they were structured and the way they did things. Their legitimacy, in other words, could no longer be taken for granted. It had to be proved and defended, as Edmund Burke was the first to see when in 1790 he wrote what might be called the founding document of modern conservatism, worldwide as much as British, that great polemic *Reflections on the Revolution in*

France. So if the French Revolution created the Left (and more of that later) it also, paradoxically enough, brought into existence the Right in order to combat it.

Revolution and religion

The same paradox can be seen if we look at the impact of the revolution on religion. Although nobody planned or foresaw a quarrel with the Roman Catholic Church in 1789, within a year it began to erupt, and by 1793, for the first time in the history of the world, the new state was attempting to stamp out religious practice throughout its territory. Secularism was born. That extreme phase only lasted a few months; but even when it ended the revolution-aries declared that the republic had no religion and favoured none; and that is a tradition which runs very deep to this day in French life. Only recently French state education looked as if it might be brought to a standstill by a dispute in which teachers objected to having Muslim girls in their class wearing religious head dress. The example has spread steadily since the French Revolution, and countries like this one are nowadays relatively unusual in having an established church and, however powerless it is in everyday terms, a state religion. Only the recent resurgence of Muslim fundamentalism, resulting in a number of Islamic republics, has reversed the trend in certain parts of the world. But it is unlikely to be imitated in western countries. All *ancien regime* states had state religions. Most modern ones do not. That is the measure of the revolution's legacy; and although it is true that the United States was technically the first country to declare itself without religious affiliations, the example which all nineteenth and twentieth-century states to have done so have followed is the French one: because the Americans took that course in response to their own religious diversity, whereas the French were driven to that position by the explosive potential of religion as demonstrated in its alliance with counter-revolution. Religion seemed to be the sworn enemy of revolutions, and since so many states now trace their ancestry back to a revolution of some form or another, it is natural that they wish to dissociate themselves from it. The extent to which they have done so, of course, has varied. Most have merely declared them-selves religiously neutral, tolerating all systems of belief and dis-criminating against none. Others, and most notably communist states, have taken a higher profile and declared themselves posi-tively hostile to all religion. The attitude goes back to the dechris-tianisation of the Jacobin republic in 1793, which communist historians celebrate as the first attempt in history systematically to uproot the forces of bigotry and superstition which had for so long helped to keep humankind in ignorance. Nor have communist regimes been wrong to proceed in this way, as the powerful religious element in much of what has occurred recently in Eastern Europe shows. Revolutionary regimes and religion don't easily mix, and never have.

No wonder, therefore, that when Napoleon did a deal with the Pope in 1802 to restore the Catholic Church in France, many people saw it as the end of the revolution. In many senses it was, because it brought to an end the conflict which had done more than anything to perpetuate division within the country. But it did not close the religious question in France: it made it a central issue in French politics for a century to come. Upto 1905 the Church constantly tried to build on its links with the state, re-established in 1802, to influence education, discussion of public affairs, and national life generally. It tended to be supported in this by monarchical regimes, which saw organised religion as a pillar of order and social subordination. Those who looked back to the revolution and republicanism for inspiration, meanwhile, fought bitterly against these tendencies, and dreamed of disestablishing the church once more as had happened between 1794 and 1802. With the triumph of republicanism after the 1870s, their moment came at last, and in the early years of this century the link was at last broken, and the revolutionary tradition at last triumphed.

Did the French Revolution therefore weaken the Church? It might look like it, but look again. One reason why the revolutionaries ran into a quarrel with it was that they miscalculated its strength, and particularly that of the papacy. In the 1780s, in fact, a lot of people thought that the Pope was finished, and his power a thing of the past. The quarrel with the revolution, however, showed that it was still a reality. The Pope's condemnation of the revolution proved crucial in the break. And when Napoleon sought to resolve the quarrel, he went straight to Rome to do it, recognising the papacy as the only authority able to make deals on behalf of the church, and backing the Pope in a sweeping purge of the old episcopacy in order to achieve it. So what the revolutionary experience actually did, so far from weakening the church, was immeasureably to strengthen the Pope's authority within it, and lay the basis of nineteenth-century claims to infallibility which earlier popes had often dreamed of, but never dared to proclaim as dogma in the way that was now done. And if the church could now no longer, in a world of religious toleration, claim the automatic and unquestioning obedience and allegiance of everybody, those whose allegiance it did receive gave it as a deliberate and conscious choice, because they *believed* the message it preached, and were thereby more committed supporters of its cause and beliefs. And so spiritually, as well as institutionally, the legacy of the revolution might well have been to make the church stronger rather than weaker, although first appearances were to the contrary.

Shift in sovereignty

Certainly those who saw themselves as the Revolution's heirs did not underestimate its resilience. It took them a century to reverse Napoleon's religious restoration, a century of often bitter struggle. But if the power of the Church sums up much of what they were against, what were they *for*? What was the revolutionary creed which the 1790s bequeathed to the nineteenth century and beyond?

First of all it was the belief that government should be *representative*. The people of 1789 saw themselves as overthrowing what they called despotism, and what historians are more inclined to label absolute monarchy: the rule of a single person unconstrained by representative institutions. Of course this principle was certainly not new. The government of Great Britain had been parliamentary for over a century, so had that of the Dutch Republic, Sweden, Poland, and a number of lesser states, not to mention the thirteen colonies of North America who saw themselves as revolting against George III in order to protect already existing representative institutions. But the ideology of the French Revolution went beyond institutions peculiar to particular countries. It said that *only* representative government is legitimate, *anywhere*. And that is because sovereignty, the ultimate, final power in any system, *always* lies with the people or the nation. No individual can be sovereign. Those exercising executive power only have the right to do so for and on behalf of the wider political community, who must confer that power by recognised procedures, regularly renewed. Thus revolutionaries, or those who saw themselves as the Revolution's heirs, always claimed to speak in the name of the people, and to be acting in their best interests. It is no coincidence that communist regimes call themselves peoples' democracies, or indeed that those who have dismantled them in Eastern Europe claimed also to be acting in the peoples' name. Even military *coups* are normally carried out ostensibly to save the nation (wherever it is) from corrupt politicians who are deemed to be betraying it: that tradition started, indeed, in 1799 when Napoleon overthrew the last regime of the French Revolution itself. The hypocrisy of such claims to representativeness is of course barefaced; but as is often said, hypocrisy is the homage that vice renders to virtue, and the important point is that those who hold, or seize power, have always felt obliged, ever since the French Revolution, to declare themselves representative because the people, or the nation, are universally recognised as the only true source of political authority.

But where does that leave kings, who upto 1789 usually claim that they derived their authority from above rather than from below, from God in fact? Initially, of course, the French Revolution was not anti-monarchical. Despite abundant and increasing evidence that Louis XVI hated the revolution and deplored the direction in which it was going, the men of 1789 were committed to establishing a constitutional monarchy. But with sovereignty now firmly located in the nation, the King could never again be a sovereign in the old sense; and it became increasingly clear that government could be carried on perfectly well without him. And so it was relatively easy to get rid of him in 1792, and the France that fought against the whole of Europe for the rest of that decade was a republic, which saw all kings as its sworn enemies. From 1792 onwards, the French revolutionary ideology was a republican one; and whenever, throughout the nineteenth century, men of the left took power, in France or elsewhere, the establishment of a republic was one of their most natural and first instincts, whether we are talking about 1848, or 1870. Indeed, much of our picture of the revolution was formed by the people of the Third Republic, who throughout the last quarter of the nineteenth century sought to justify the regime they had established by appealing to the traditions passed down from the First Republic. It was then that the history of the revolution was first established as a serious academic subject, that the struggle against a state church reached its climax and was brought to a successful conclusion, and that the imagery of the revolution finally established itself as part of the paraphernalia of the state. One of the few things everybody knows about the revolution is that its motto was *Liberty, Equality, Fraternity*, and if you go to France even today you can find it everywhere – on coins, on public notices, and on public buildings. But in fact that famous trio was only the motto of the First Republic between 1793 and 1795 and not the whole revolution; and it only came into general use as the slogan of the French state when that state became firmly and finally republican in the 1870s. But it was all part of an attempt to emphasise that in the revolutionary legacy there was no place for kings, or indeed emperors.

Social equality

It was not simply that representative regimes did not need them – although they don't. The monarchy only survives in a country like Britian, and, indeed, those other Western countries where they still have crowned heads, because it has no power and is therefore incapable of going against the elected government which embodies the true source of sovereignty, the national will. But monarchy was not just a political authority of no legitimacy; it was also a symbol of other things, *social* things, which the revolutionary ideology and the revolutionary tradition also rejected as the antithesis of something they were emphatically for: *Equality*. All men are born, says the Declaration of the Rights of Man, and remain, free and equal in rights. That means that nobody should have any automatic privilege, precedence or advantage recognised by the law. Everybody should have access to every available opportunity according to their abilities and their talents. Now, monarchy is a complete negation of this. Why should anybody inherit power or authority by the accident of birth? And if the state is dedicated to equality of opportunity, how much more important is it that the headship of the state should be accessible to all on the same terms? That's one more reason for having a republic. But the principle applies far more widely than this. Equality means no aristocracy, no hereditary superiority or privilege. This principle was present in the French Revolution from the start, and thousands of nobles emigrated from the country during its first few years in order to escape from it. But nobility did not disappear from French society. Napoleon revived it with a vengeance, the restored Bourbons perpetuated it, and so did Napoleon III. It was only with the advent of the Third Republic that the French state finally abandoned the creation of hereditary distinctions – another sign of the revolution's final triumph after 1870. And meanwhile nobles everywhere, like kings, had no illusions about what the triumph of French revolutionary principles would mean for them. When Lady Bracknell in *The Importance of Being Earnest* deplored the worst excesses of the French Revolution and declared that we all know what that unfortunate movement led to, what she meant (I suppose) was what it led to for aristocrats like her. After 1789, the writing was on the wall for nobilities everywhere: and although they fought a spirited rearguard action which we might argue is not quite over even now, it *has* been a defensive one. Over those two centuries, by and large the principle of civil equality has triumphed.

Economic equality

But, of course, there are more forms of equality than that. What about economic equality? Here the French Revolution was a lot more ambiguous. In the Declaration, *property* was also proclaimed one of the natural rights of man, and that was basically a principle of inequality. Soon afterwards participation in representative government was made to depend on a property, whether as a voter or a repesentative, and that certainly meant that some citizens were more equal than others. And that principle, too, held good right upto the Third Republic, when manhood suffrage eventually arrived. But right from the start it was also challenged. If men were born equal and retained equal rights, some said, there *must* be economic equality, too, or the whole idea was a mockery. That meant first of all no property qualifications for voting or any sort of political participation: that was achieved by 1792. Then it meant economic controls to ensure that everybody had access to decent subsistence. This too was tried in 1793 and 1794. And for some it also meant other things: a shareout of property, if not indeed the abolition of private property altogether. These things were never tried, but they were talked about, dreamed about, and plotted for. And during that time, the early years of the first republic, the *sansculottes* of Paris elaborated a programme of popular power by which such things might be achieved. After all, if the people were sovereign, surely that meant the majority who had little or no property? None of this passed without challenge during the revolution, but nevertheless it too established a tradition, or rather traditions, of popular power in states and society – the traditions that were to come together in the course of the nineteenth century under the general label of socialism. Socialism is about popular power, and about social equality as well as political equality. Whether that can be achieved alongside private property or whether the abolition of such property is an essential prerequisite, is what divides ordinary socialists from communists; but they are united in looking back to the French Revolution as the first time in history when the ideals and aspirations they stand for were expressed, and sometimes tried. It is no coincidence that most of the historians who have worked on the *sansculottes*, or on the Jacobin phase of the First Republic in 1793–4, or on Babeuf's egalitarian conspiracy of 1796, have been men of the far left looking for the historical roots of their own beliefs. Without the French Revolution we would have had no socialism and no communism – which is perhaps why Thatcher hated the thought of it.

National freedom

Is, then, the collapse of communism, which we have recently witnessed in so many countries, the end, after two centuries, of the revolution's legacy, the end, indeed, of the revolution itself? It certainly seems to mark the rejection of some of the types of regime whose first ancestors can be found in France in the 1790s: irreligious, one-party republics claiming to represent the people and dedicated to social equality, and claiming themselves to be products of revolution. But when one looks at what has happened, what is striking is how far those who have turned against these communist regimes *also* represent French revolutionary traditions. They saw *themselves* as revolutionaries, driving excitedly through the streets waving tricolours, the flag of freedom first flown in 1789. In Tiananmen Square in 1989 they sang the *Marseillaise*, the hymn of liberty. They were attacking the communist regimes for *betraying* revolutionary ideals, and not because those ideals were no longer believed in and they wanted to re-establish kings and aristocracies. And apart from resentment at injustice, the new inequality of privileges enjoyed only by party members, a fundamental driving force of these fascinating and exciting developments was *Nationalism* – a creed, or rather an attitude of mind, that can also be traced back to revolutionary France, like so many other things that are still with us.

Further Reading

Doyle, W. *The Oxford History of the French Revolution* (Oxford University Press, 1989) Chapter 17.
Hobsbawm, E.J. *Echoes of the Marseillaise* (Rutgers, 1990).
Rice, E.E. (ed.) *Revolution and Counter-Revolution* (Basil Blackwell, 1991).
McManners, J. *Church and State in France 1870–1914* (SPCK, 1972).
Wilson, E. *To the Finland Station* (Fontana 1960).
Kedourie, E. *Nationalism* (Hutchinson, 1966).

Professor William Doyle teaches in the School of History at the University of Bristol.

John Derry
Castlereagh's Foreign Policy

Castlereagh was the principal architect of the final defeat of Napoleon, although he was less successful in shaping post-war Europe. There was also considerable continuity between his policy and that of successors such as Canning and Palmerston.

Castlereagh's presuppositions about foreign policy were rooted in experience going right back to the 1790s. First of all it is important to remember that he was by background an Irishman. His early political experience was gained in Ireland. He had experience both as a reformer in Ireland and as Irish Secretary. He was involved in the repression of the Irish rebellion of 1798 and in carrying the Act of Union in 1800–1. And this Irish experience is important, because it undoubtedly gave him an insight, which perhaps an Englishman lacked, into the problem of persuading or cajoling different communities to coexist together. Whether he was successful in doing that in Ireland is of course questionable, but it is important to mention it.

Pitt's influence

The second point I want to emphasise at the start is that the whole of his foreign policy must be judged against the background and the influence of the Younger Pitt. Like George Canning, Castlereagh was very much the protégé of the Younger Pitt, brought forward by Pitt into prominent public office. And he was undoubtedly influenced, throughout the period when he was Foreign Secretary, by an important memorandum which William Pitt had drawn up in January 1805. At that time Pitt was seeking to create the third coalition against revolutionary and imperial France. He defined the main objectives of British policy which he hoped would be accepted by the coalition allies. The first policy was to confine France within ancient limits, which in 1805 and indeed in 1814, came to mean the frontiers of 1792, on the eve of the outbreak of the great European war. Because of the hundred days, that aim was amended at the Congress of Vienna to mean the frontiers of 1790, but the principle was the same, to confine France within ancient limits.

Pitt's second aim was to strengthen the countries on the borders of France to act as a deterrent against a renewal of French aggression. Undoubtedly, the peacemakers in 1814–15 bore that in mind. Thirdly, and this is in a sense the germ of the Congress System, Pitt stated that at the end of the war it would be desirable to try to create in Europe a system of mutual protection and security, which would guarantee the integrity of sovereign states and help to create what he called 'public law' in Europe. We mean by that 'international law'. In other words, it was an attempt to extend into peace the experience of war. If Napoleon, say, could be defeated only by a coalition, perhaps collaboration between powers was the best way of ensuring that in future there would not be a great European war.

Now of course it laid that down only in the most general terms, but we have in Castlereagh's correspondence an actual reference to that memorandum, where he said that he often thought back to Pitt's memorandum, and in 1805 we also know that Castlereagh had long discussions with Pitt about the conduct of policy and the evolution of Britain's war aims.

A third experience which he brought to the conduct of foreign affairs was of course his important experience as War Secretary, especially during the period of the Portland administration 1807–9. It is now generally agreed that despite the disappointment of the Walcheren expedition, and the fact that the Portland ministry collapsed over this in considerable rancour, typified by the famous duel between Castlereagh and George Canning, Castlereagh's conduct at the War Office undoubtedly set forth guidelines for the future conduct of war, the creation of an expeditionary force and, most important of all, laid the foundations for military success in the Iberian peninsula.

So when in 1812 he became Foreign Secretary and leader of the House of Commons in Lord Liverpool's administration, these are the things that he brought to the examination of the problems he faced. And he faced a great many problems. Don't fall into the trap of thinking that history is predetermined. It is only with hindsight that we can see that in 1812 the war was bound to turn in favour of the Allies. Until Napoleon's retreat from Russia nobody quite knew how the war would end, and that was true despite the success of the British, Spaniards and Portuguese, in particular the campaign of 1812 in Spain. Although Wellington did liberate Madrid, he eventually had to return to Portugal and it was only the campaign of 1813 which eventually evicted the French from Spain.

Building the final coalition

So when Castlereagh looked at the problems he faced, the first one was to try, particularly after Napoleon's defeat in Russia, to build up an effective coalition against France. This was an exercise Pitt and Grenville had gone through on three previous occasions. What's important here is the added sensitivity which Castlereagh brought to that task. It is important to remember that in 1813 Austria was reluctant to enter the war against Napoleon. There were good reasons for that. Despite the defeat in Russia, Metternich was afraid that Napoleon might recover his balance, and he was also anxious about Russian and Prussian influence in eastern and central Europe. This anxiety was something that Metternich and Castlereagh shared right through the war years, the post-war years, and into the early 1820s when they sought to deal with the problems caused by the Greek revolt against the Turkish sultan. Castlereagh observed, that in order to defeat Napoleon, 'we need great masses'. He recognised that they needed the Russians' steamroller. But he also recognised that the problem was not to persuade the Tsar to march his armies into other countries, but to persude him to march them out again.

The alliance was fraught with many difficulties. The war aims of Prussia, Russia and Britain were not necessarily synonymous, and when eventually Austria did throw in its lot with the alliance, chiefly because Napoleon rejected a peace offer, it was quite clear that Austria likewise had deep anxieties about whether the price of defeat of France would be the assertion of Russian and Prussian power in Europe. This explains why frequently Britain and Austria tended to act together, but that was not true initially. What made Castlereagh distinctive among British politicians was that he was prepared to accept and to admit that from the Austrian point of view, entry into the war was far from obvious. And he therefore argued that instead of trying to cajole or goad Austria into joining the alliance, careful persuasion was necessary.

Having created the alliance, the second problem was to keep it in being. Again, it is only in retrospect that the defeat of Napoleon in 1814 seems inevitable. In the end, despite defeats such as Leipzig in 1813, Napoleon seemed at least partly to restore his military fortunes, and after every check he inflicted upon the allied armies in central Europe and northern France there was a tendency for the allies to squabble among themselves over whether after all they were going to defeat the greatest military genius of the age. Here Castlereagh's contribution was absolutely decisive, because in the winter of 1813–14 he journeyed to Europe, went to Basle and met the envoys from Austria, Prussia and Russia. It was through Castlereagh's own personal approach that the alliance reaffirmed that it would fight on and defeat the French and that there would be no secondary peace with France on the part of individual members of the alliance and that Britain would pledge to continue to subsidise the cost of the armies of British allies. There is no doubt that Castlereagh's personal intervention helped hold the line at a crucial stage just as the impact of Wellington's victories, first in Spain and then in southern France, heartened the allies in the closing stages of the war.

Diplomatic skills

This is a reminder that Castlereagh was particularly skilful in the art of personal diplomacy. Jokes were often made about Castlereagh's defects as a public speaker and in the House of Commons. Even as close a friend as the Duke of Wellington once said: 'Castlereagh had a great deal of ability and skill, except the skill of speaking in the House of Commons'. There are even books today which quote some of the convoluted sentences in which Castlereagh indulged in his Commons speeches, about the allies turning their backs upon themselves and this sort of thing. It is odd because in his early years in the Irish House of Commons he was well-known as an effective speaker. But if he had limitations as a public speaker, he was remarkably skilful in dealing with MPs and with foreign diplomats. There is no doubt that he had the skills that he often required as government leader in the House of Commons. Anyone coming into face-to-face negotiation with Castlereagh found firstly that he was well-briefed, secondly that he was extremely courteous, and thirdly that he was extremely shrewd in day-to-day negotiations.

This is an important element in the relationship built up at first with Metternich and then, at least at times, with the great Talleyrand, the man who had survived all the upheavals of French Revolution and Empire, serving the Revolution, then Napoleon and then at the end the Bourbons. And there is no doubt that at Vienna, Austria and Britain found it convenient to work with defeated France in order to seek bounds to the power exercised by Prussia and Russia. Castlereagh's personal skills as negotiator and diplomat were particularly important in this situation. Then of course, in looking at the terms of peace, he was quite certain that no punitive peace, so far as France was concerned, made sense. The powers liked to differentiate between defeating Napoleon and punishing France. Though in the end the French defeat was total, in fact France escaped remarkably lightly. Even after Waterloo, France was only required to retreat to the 1790 frontiers.

The Congress of Vienna

Castlereagh, like most British politicians, was convinced there could be no lasting peace with Napoleon. It was not true that Britain fought the war purely to oppose Napoleon. If Napoleon had been reasonable about peace terms Britain would have accepted peace with France. But there is no doubt that by 1814, British political opinion, with the exception of a handful of opposition Whigs, was clear that Napoleon had to go and that the only viable alternative to Napoleon was the restoration of the Bourbons in the person of Louis XVIII. Castlereagh was strongly opposed to one other suggestion which had been floated from time to time, that there should be some form of regency on the part of Napoleon's little son, the King of Rome. Even more, Castlereagh disliked the suggestion that any other leader should be imposed on France, such as the Crown Prince of Sweden, a former Marshal of France. Bernadotte actually thought he might be the better successor to the throne, but so far as Britain was concerned that was unacceptable. There is no doubt that whilst the principle of legitimacy was not seen as essential, a restoration of the Bourbons seemed the least objectionable policy.

His other anxieties were to procure a reasonable balance in the territorial arrangements which followed the war. Here he had to face some disappointment. There was a problem with Poland, for example. Poland, partitioned by Austria, Prussia and Russia three times in the closing decades of the eighteenth century, partly restored during the wars, in a slimmed-down form as the Grand Duchy of Warsaw, had in 1815 effectively been given back to Russia. The Tsar was made King of Poland. It was meant to be a separate crown, but relatively quickly Poland became part of the empire of all the Russias. The Polish problem is an important one because the success of the Russians in getting hold of Poland meant that Prussia was eager for compensation to balance Russian gains. There were discussions about the problem of Saxony. The Prussians even suggested that the Kingdom of Saxony should be eliminated. That was unacceptable to Austria and Britain and eventually what happened was that about a third of Saxony was given to Prussia, but the Kingdom of Saxony survived. The Saxons had made the mistake of remaining too loyal to Napoleon for too long. They didn't change sides in time.

Another problem was that of Norway, because in the closing stages of the war against France, Castlereagh had felt that it was important to bring Sweden into the coalition and the price of that was virtually promising the Swedes that the Danes would lose Norway and there would be a new union of crowns between Norway and Sweden. That was criticised by the opposition in the British House of Commons, but the union between Norway and Sweden lasted until 1905.

In terms of colonial gains, of course, Britain did quite well, collecting additional West Indian islands, the Cape of Good Hope and Ceylon. This is a reminder that unlike the European powers, British foreign policy was just as concerned with global and commercial matters as with the balance of power in Europe. The other point to remember about the treaty is that Castlereagh worked very hard to try to persuade the other powers at Vienna to abolish the slave trade. The slave trade had only been abolished in 1807 in the British Empire. The real obstacle to the abolition of the slave trade was the suspicion of the Spaniards and Portuguese that, by abolishing the slave trade, Britain was simply trying to break into Latin American markets. There was at least an element of truth in that. The Spanish and Portuguese deeply resented suggestions, for example, that the Royal Navy should inspect vessels to see if they were carrying slaves. The position was made more complicated by the fact that during the hundred days Napoleon had abolished the slave trade in France in his attempt to create a more liberal image. That abolition was accepted by the restored Bourbons. Of course Austria, Prussia and Russia had very little interest in the slave trade. Spain and Portugal were the problem. It is very interesting to look at letters which Castlereagh wrote, proving beyond any doubt whatsoever that this alleged reactionary worked very hard in the end to persuade the powers either to abolish the slave trade or to control it in the interests of humanity.

The Congress System

The other thing which emerges from Vienna is the growing belief that if one Congress had worked well, then perhaps Congresses should be a regular pattern of international relations. Care should be taken not to identify this with anything like the United Nations or the League of Nations or even anything like the European Union. Even those who advocated Congresses were unsure whether they should meet at fixed intervals or only when there was a recognisable threat to peace. Castlereagh felt that since diplomacy had been an important part of first winning the war and then settling the peace, that it would be expedient if the powers met from time to time in order to monitor or scrutinise inevitable change. I put it that way because Castlereagh never believed that the peace settlement of 1815 should be unchangeable in every respect. As he once said in another context: 'Nothing in our system is absolutely unchangeable.'

It was true of course that he was cautious about embarking on any ambitious programme of liberalisation; he was prepared to see a constitutional monarchy established in France and in Spain, but he realised that particularly in Germany the institution of liberalism would prove far from easy. But he did believe that each nation would inevitably evolve at its own pace and in its own way. In other words the sort of balance of power or equilibrium that he had in mind was essentially a balance of power between the sovereign states of Europe, leaving their internal institutions and their internal developments to change at their own rate. This is why Castlereagh was always opposed to any policy of collective intervention in the internal affairs of sovereign states.

Now of course, that attitude is perfectly explicable coming from the foreign minister of a constitutional, parliamentary state whose interests were primarily colonial and commercial. Metternich, as the Chancellor of a multi-national, multi-ethnic, multi-religious, multi-linguistic empire which had only one bond of unity, the Habsburg dynasty, was bound to regard things rather differently. And there is no doubt that the two men perceived equilibrium in rather different ways right from the start, although that was not immediately obvious. It worked for them though, since the holy alliance eventually became Metternich's chosen vehicle for a policy of collective intervention and repression.

The Holy Alliance

It is worth remembering that originally Metternich was sceptical about the Holy Alliance. The original holy alliance was not Metternich's idea, it was an idea of Tsar Alexander. Now Tsar Alexander of Russia was in some ways the most powerful man in Europe. He was also very erratic, apt to swing almost daily from being curiously liberal and idealistic to being repressive and highly reactionary. He was a man who was also prey to huge religious enthusiasm; for example, during his visit to Paris at the end of the Napoleonic war, Tsar Alexander closeted himself with a well-known religious mystic. This caused amusement amongst the other diplomats in Paris at the time. And the idea of the Holy Alliance was originally that the kings of Europe should agree to treat each other as Christian brothers and to rule their peoples on principles of Christian benevolence.

Now how you put practical political meaning to those phrases is of course highly questionable. Alexander was sincere: the other diplomats thought it was crazy. Castlereagh described it in a letter to Lord Liverpool as a piece of sublime mysticism and nonsense. But he still thought they might have to humour the Tsar. Likewise, initially Metternich thought the scheme was idiotic but that in the long term it was necessary to humour the Tsar. It was only when the Tsar swung to the right and when in Prussia and France there were also marked shifts to the right in terms of domestic policy, that Metternich realised that an alliance of sovereigns could perhaps do what the Congress System was failing to do.

This was at the root of the growing British alienation from the other members of the Concert of Europe. Now this is not to say that

Congresses were failing. The peace settlement of 1815 was a remarkable success, for it effectively gave Europe 100 years of peace. I don't think many historians today would take absolutely seriously those familiar textbook criticisms that it was a bad peace because, for instance, it ignored liberalism and nationalism. We are more and more aware that in the circumstances the terms nationalist and liberal were a) hardly defined and b) infinitely more uncertain in terms of their practical meaning than we might think.

Breakdown of the Congress System

The Congress of Aix-la-Chapelle in 1818 was also a success, that effectively re-anchored France to the rest of Europe. The occupying forces were withdrawn, the French had paid their indemnity and France became a full member of the alliance. The problem really began in 1820. It was brought to a head by revolution in Spain, and Naples, in other parts of Italy, and troubles in Poland. As a result of this, Metternich, in alliance with Russia, Prussia and France, was eager to embark on a policy of collective intervention, particularly in Naples and perhaps in Spain. This provoked Britain's response, Castlereagh's famous statement, made in 1820 and again in the famous British Circular of 1821, where he stated that Britain could not support collective intervention in the internal affairs of sovereign states. Intervention was only legitimate where a power or combination of powers was threatening the peace of Europe by threatening to mount aggression against a neighbour. That was unacceptable from Metternich's point of view because of course he was worried about the effect of liberal ideas in one part of Europe having a knock-on effect in Austria.

And this means that by Castlereagh's suicide in 1822, Britain had become isolated. There is no doubt that if Castlereagh had lived, Britain would have broken the links with the Congress System and with the other powers in Europe. The difference would have been that whereas George Canning embarked on that new departure as he liked to think of it, with enthusiasm, Castlereagh would have embarked upon it more in sorrow than in anger, because it represented the end of the hope that the Congress System would be able to maintain peace. Remember at the heart of this is a crucial difference between a man like Castlereagh who saw conferences between the powers as a means of monitoring and accepting change, whilst minimising the risk to peace and stability, and Metternich's more rigid attitude. Remember that Castlereagh did not attend those later conferences in person; Britain was represented by his half-brother, the third Marquis of Londonderry. The Duke of Wellington was also prominent as one of Britain's representatives. But the Congress System as envisaged by Castlereagh, failed to materialise.

Policy towards South America

There are one or two other areas which I would like to highlight in terms of foreign policy. The first is Castlereagh's attitude to Latin America. You will be aware that George Canning recognised the independence of the Latin American republics who had revolted against Spain. The famous phrase about 'calling the New World into existence to redress the balance of the Old' sums up what George Canning claimed he was doing. But recognising the independence of the Latin American republics was actually seen as a possibility by Castlereagh as early as 1808, before any of those colonies had formally rebelled against Spain. The background to this is, of course, Napoleon's intervention in Portugal, and his attempt to impose his brother Joseph on the throne of Spain. This created a situation in which Castlereagh said that the time might come when it would be in Britain's interests to recognise the independence of the Spanish American republics. That was still in his mind when tension grew between the Spanish American colonies and the restored Bourbons in Spain. Castlereagh had no time for the Spanish Bourbons. He constantly lamented that if Spanish liberals and radicals were unrealistic, the reactionaries in Spain were as ignorant. He felt that Spain was a country torn by factions, both of which were unreasonable.

But he was prepared to compromise across the range of independence. First *de facto*, possibly eventually *de jure*, recognition was contemplated. Now, his motives were not specifically philanthropic or idealistic. He had in mind not merely the fact that the domestic regime in Spain was oppressive, but that if Britain were the friend of these young Latin American republics, it would enable the British to do what they had been trying to do for centuries and break effectively into the Latin American market. He was just as interested in exploiting the situation in Latin America for the defence of British interests and for the stimulation of British commerce as he was concerned about domestic politics in Spain or the type of regime in Bolivia. So although there was a difference in rhetoric, there was actually considerable continuity in the foreign policies of Castlereagh and Canning, despite the famous rivalry between the two.

Anglo-American relations

A second area of importance in throwing light on Castlereagh's conduct of foreign policy is Anglo-American relations. An American historian, Professor Bradford Perkins, has gone so far as to say that

Castlereagh was the first British minister fully to come to terms with the long-term consequences of American independence, and what that meant for the balance of power and the future role of North America. I think he may be exaggerating; it is possible to say that Lord Shelburne or Lord Grenville had some appreciation of what American independence meant. But the argument is essentially sound. Unlike many other British politicians of the time, Castlereagh valued good Anglo-American relations as something desirable in their own right. He once went on to say that there were no two nations which were more closely bound together, despite the quarrels of the past and the war of 1812, than the United States and Britain. The war of 1812 was caused partly by American resentment over the effects of the Britsh blockade on commerce, partly by their resentment at Britain's claim to search neutral ships at sea for contraband goods and for British seamen, and of course partly too by the ambition of some Americans for the conquest of Canada. The war was a singularly messy and unhappy one. It was an indecisive draw. The American invasion of Canada failed, the sea fights on the Great Lakes were pretty well inconclusive, though some of them may have shocked British national pride. Though the British did occupy Washington, they were defeated at New Orleans.

Now Castlereagh's attitude to this war was that it was best ended as soon as possible. His approach at the peace negotiations in Ghent, (which he did not take part in personally because at that time he was fully occupied in the negotiations I mentioned earlier with the major powers of Europe), was that the British negotiators should seek peace and that they should in fact defer some of the more controversial issues simply in order to get peace. He tore up tough Foreign Office plans and substituted more conciliatory ones of his own. This conciliatory policy was continued right through to his death in 1822. For example, when some American prisoners of war were killed in a prisoner-of-war camp he apologised to the Americans and offered compensation. When some American seamen and British seamen got into a brawl in Gibraltar he showed the same conciliatory attitude. He was also conciliatory over controversial issues such as fishing off Newfoundland. On matters connected with the Great Lakes, he favoured a policy which would see Britain and America reducing military and naval forces to an absolute minimum. As far as the future boundary between Canada and the United States was concerned, although this wasn't settled until the 1840s, Castlereagh favoured what eventually came to pass, that west of the Great Lakes, the 49th parallel should be accepted as the boundary between Canada and the United States. This was the backdrop against which Canning's famous adage about the New World must be judged.

The Greek revolt

Then there is the important question of the Greek revolt. The handling of this was very complex, because of the problems it created for the powers. There was a great deal of sentimental support for the Greeks and against the Turks, partly of course because many educated people drenched in the old classical education romanticised the Greeks. Castlereagh himself said that though every educated man must sympathise with the Greeks, it was important to remember that 90% of the Greeks were not the same as the ancient Greeks. The problem for Castlereagh and Metternich was their mutual suspicion that Russia would seek to exploit the Greek revolt. Neither of them particularly liked the Ottoman Empire, but they feared that if it collapsed, Russian influence would grow in the Balkans and in eastern Europe. Castlereagh and Metternich both tried to work on the Tsar and tell him that he shouldn't really support the Greeks in revolt against the Sultan, who was after all a legitimate monarch. Only when that approach had clearly failed did they begin to edge towards some form of collaboration and intervention, allegedly to protect the Greeks, but actually to prevent Russian expansion. Both the British and the French were deeply anxious about Russia and there is no doubt that distrust of Russia was one of the constant themes in Castlereagh's handling of foreign policy. In the end you might argue that this goes back to the eighteenth century. In 1791 the Younger Pitt had tried to check the Empress Catherine in her expansionist designs on the Black Sea. He failed, partly because the Prussians wouldn't support him. But this distrust of Russia, which of course was mainstream British foreign policy until the early twentieth century, was one of the important themes in Castlereagh's conduct of foreign policy. It is the foreign policy of a man who saw politics not in the light of ideals but as managing conflicting interests in such a way as to minimise threats to peace and maximise the harmony of nations. This means that he didn't seek anything Utopian as the aim of foreign policy, but aimed at producing a balance of power which would preserve peace. That balance included change, because change is an inevitable element in all political development. In his defence of British interests he set the course for British foreign policy continued by Canning. Palmerston and Salisbury through the rest of the nineteenth century.

Further Reading

Bartlett, C.J. *Castlereagh* (1966).
Bridge, F.R. and Bullen, R. *The Great Powers and the European States System 1815–1914* (1981).
Dakin, D. *The Greek Struggle for Independence, 1821–33* (1973).
Derry, J.W. *Castlereagh* (1976).
Hinde, W. *Castlereagh* (1981).
Kissinger, H. *A World Restored: Metternich, Castlereagh and the Problems of Peace, 1815–22* (1957).
Seaman, L.C.B. *From Vienna to Versailles* (1964).
Webster, C. *The Foreign Policy of Castlereagh* (1963).

John Derry teaches History at Newcastle University.

Pamela Pilbeam
France 1814–48: Monarchy and its Enemies

Why did France have revolutions in 1830 and 1848? Was it because of a revolutionary tradition from 1789, or was it due more to the weaknesses of the state?

Why was French constitutional monarchy so unstable and short-lived in the nineteenth century? We used to be told it was because the 1789 Revolution left a ruling class at war with itself. Marxist historians, dominant in France until the 1960s, added that a republic (socialist) was the inevitable conclusion of the 'bourgeois' revolution of 1789. The collapse of Communism in Europe shot holes in the notion of the inevitable success of Marxism and revisionist historians from Cobban onwards added the weight of logic and empirical research. So where does this leave constitutional monarchy? Today and for well over 30 years, the French have apparently delighted in a presidential regime, in which the head of state has a major voice in decision-making, so there is nothing alien to the French in such systems. What were the attractions of monarchy in the first half of the nineteenth century? What were the alternatives? How was it that both royalist experiments lasted less than a generation each?

Defeat

The Bourbon Monarchy was restored by France's enemies following Napoleon's comprehensive defeat in 1814 and again after his Hundred Day return in 1815. Napoleon, not Louis XVIII, lost the war, and his Hundred Day return from Elba between March and July 1815 ensured a much harsher Second than First Treaty of Paris, but it was the Bourbons who reaped the odium of those who endured the humiliation of occupation. There was little popular support for a restored monarchy, but a settled system of government was vital. The Allies occupied 61 departments at French expense, demanded a hefty indemnity before they would leave and were determined on a royalist France. Was a monarchy doomed to be hated by the French themselves?

Constitutional compromise

The Bourbons were restored with an elected parliament and a written constitution to check their power. The framework of the modern French state, erected during the previous 25 Revolutionary and Napoleonic years and little modified even today, was preserved, including administrative, judicial, financial and educational institutions, and the Napoleonic Codes of Law. The Constitution of 1814 was a compromise, describing itself as a grant of 'royal grace and favour', whereas it was in fact the work of a committee of former Bonapartists and Royalists. A parliament was created, with a Chamber of Deputies elected by all adult males who paid at least 300 francs in direct taxes, in all about 100,000 out of a population of around 30 million. This was to share legislative power with the King, who appointed governments, whose members were described as 'responsible'. The Constitution proclaimed individual liberal freedoms of religion and opinion, while restoring Catholicism as the State Church. The Revolutionary Land Settlement, purchases of Church and *emigré* land during the 1790s, were guaranteed. This constitution, revised modestly after the 1830 Revolution was an advantage envied by foreign liberals and copied abroad in 1848. Ironically the ambiguity and the inflexibility of the document put the charter at the centre of the political conflicts which contributed to the destruction of both monarchies, the Bourbon with the July Revolution of 1830 and the Orleanist in the February Revolution of 1848.

Enemies of monarchy

1 Bonapartism

Napoleon died on St Helena in 1821; his son, barely 10 years old and in poor health, was reared as an Austrian by his mother's family. The absence of a Bonapartist candidate allowed sentimental Bonapartism to flourish among Napoleon's former soldiers and public servants, especially those excluded from office after they had rallied to the Emperor during the Hundred Days. The 1830 Revolution gave them back their jobs, but they were happy to settle for a constitutional monarch. Napoleon's great-nephew, Louis-Napoleon, made two farcical attempts to seize power; at Strasbourg in 1836 and Boulogne in 1840. The local garrisons showed little interest, despite his *Napoleonic Ideas*, published in 1839, in which he tried to prove that Napoleon had been a constitutional ruler at heart. Bonapartism retained considerable popularity, both at élite and mass levels, revelling in the memory of the military hegemony, obliterating the defeat; creating a myth of Imperial economic greatness, forgetting the disastrous economic costs of war. Louis-Philippe tried to acquire reflected glory by heading the successful campaign for the return of the Emperor's ashes to Paris and their re-burial at *Les Invalides* in 1840. He never succeeded in making Bonapartism Orleanist, but nor did Bonapartism itself emerge as a specific political movement until after the June Days in 1848.

2 Republican conspiracy

There was no future in being republican in 1814–15 and there were only a few committed republicans on the eve of 1848. A specific republican movement developed in response to the consequences of the 1830 Revolution among those who had hoped for more, either personally or politically from the former liberals who hoisted themselves to power. The movement was small; the Society of the Rights of Man had about 3,000 members in 1833, compared with the 60,000 or so adherents of the *charbonnerie* in the early 1820s. Its members were journalists, disillusioned Restoration liberals, young idealists, including some lawyers, doctors, and junior army officers. Republicans wanted an electorate broader then that of the July Monarchy, although precisely how democratic was never really determined. They championed the physical and moral welfare of the poor in a rather paternalistic fashion. Republican doctors like Raspail, Trélat and Guépin ran free clinics. Republicans ran evening classes in basic literacy in Paris, Lyon and other large towns. They stressed that the republic was a peaceful, long-term goal.

Republicans were also conspirators. Members of the many small republican clubs were ordered to supply themselves with weapons and drill regularly. There were a number of minor skirmishes with the Orleanist regime between 1831 and 1834 which stimulated sufficient panic in the latter to provoke a total ban on all political associations in 1834 and on the lively republican press a year later. Daumier had to turn from political to social targets. Even the word 'republican' was banned. Conspiracy persisted, but in a very minor vein. The irrepressible insurgent, Auguste Blanqui, organised the Society of the Families until detection in 1836 and its successor, the Society of the Seasons. Both were exclusively committed to the violent overthrow of the monarchy and the creation of an egalitarian socialist republic. Both were total disasters. Blanqui's attempted seizure of power in May 1839 fizzled out in one day, abysmally failing to engage popular support for the revolt of his vanguard party.

3 Socialism: a Utopian dream?

Industrial growth brought periodic disasters for French workers, who were predominantly artisans in these years. Anxious discussions about the urban social crisis were as common in the early nineteenth century as they are today, and about as effectual. Socialist solutions had an appeal to artisans, especially in Paris and the larger towns. The socialists of the 1830s and 1840s roundly condemned capitalist competition and the Orleanist regime for the military backing it gave to industrialists. But socialists could not agree on how to solve the problems. Blanqui was isolated in his revolutionary convictions. Some, like Louis Blanc, proposed that the state should provide loans to artisans to set up co-operative workshops. Others, like Etienne Cabet, put their faith in co-operation, not class war between artisans and the bourgeoisie. Cabet himself soon lapsed into a rather ineffectual utopianism. Then there were men such as Fourier and Proudhon, who suggested that self-governing small communes could replace the centralised state. The impact of socialist ideas made a republic even more remote, talk of radical social change alarmed those for whom a purely political, even democratic, republic might have been tolerable.

Why revolution?

If the opponents of constitutional royalism were so divided and few in number, why did the two monarchical experiments fail? There are striking similarities in the outbreak of the July Revolution in 1830 and the February Revolution of 1848. In both cases political conflict was accompanied by economic crisis. In 1830 the quarrel was between the King and the liberal majority in the elected Chamber of Deputies; in 1848 the minority opposition in parliament took their argument outside the chamber in a search for political advantage. In 1829 Charles X, ultra-royalist brother of the first restored Bourbon, the more conciliatory Louis XVIII, refused to select his government to suit the politics of the liberal majority in the Chamber of Deputies, which was the norm, and appointed ultra-royalist ministers. In 1830 the chamber passed an unprecedented motion of no confidence in this Polignac government. Charles dissolved parliament and lost the election comprehensively. After some hesitation the King was persuaded that the 274 liberals in a Chamber of Deputies of 430 were a revolutionary threat and that the constitution allowed him to rule by decree in an emergency. Hence the Four Ordinances of St Cloud, (26 July 1830) dissolved parliament before it could meet, reduced the electorate to exclude all but the quarter most rich and called for new elections. The liberal opposition newspapers which had led the campaign against Polignac with striking success were to close.

Were the ordinances the catalyst or actual cause of the revolution which followed? If it had been left to the deputies, Charles X would probably have got away with the ordinances. The liberals were cautious, sober members of the élite, as keen as the King to avoid violent confrontation. They held a few timid meetings in their homes to discuss how they could survive the ordinances. The majority of the liberal journalists however, openly challenged the King's right to rule by decree and risked unrest by encouraging their employees to join demonstrations. Successful defiance came from the liberal press and artisan protests.

In 1848 the centre of gravity of the political crisis was different. The Guizot government, in office since 1840, increased its majority in the elections of 1842 and 1846 to reach 290 out of 430 deputies in 1846. There were predictable rumblings that a single group of ministers had remained in office too long. Rumours of corruption crystallised into unpleasant reality in the case of Charles Teste. Left-of-centre monarchists and republicans launched a renewed offensive in the summer of 1847. Duvergier de Hauranne campaigned for the reform of constituency boundaries, observing that demographic changes meant that tiny shrinking, agrarian constituencies in the south were safe seats for the government, while the much larger and growing constituencies in the Paris area and the industrial north elected proportionately far fewer deputies but were the stronghold of the opposition. Critics also drew attention to the large number of placemen; 40% of the chamber held official posts. Curiously this had always been so. What is odd is that Charles X could not keep his parliaments sweet, even with so much patronage to bestow.

During 1847 an opposition proposal for electoral reform was as comprehensively rejected by parliament as had been similar attempts in earlier years. The case for reform was taken to the country. In the second half of the year a series of reforming banquets were held throughout France. Banquets were traditional ways to publicise opposition. The law banned political associations, but subscription banquets, confined to a well-heeled elite prepared to pay four francs or so for the privilege of listening to political speeches, were tolerated, indeed a substantial part of the audience always consisted of public officials. When parliament resumed at the end of December 1847 the banquets continued, but their organisers could not agree on how much electoral reform was desirable. Given the government's majority, was there any more need for Guizot to concern himself?

In February 1848 permission was requested for a banquet in Paris, which, the press announced, would be accompanied by a popular march in favour of reform. After much hesitation, alarmed at the prospect of the participation of large crowds of unemployed artisans, the government banned the banquet. The demonstration itself went ahead. The attempt to check the march led directly to the demise of Louis-Philippe.

Economic crises and revolution

In both 1830 and 1848 the key to the overthrow of the monarchy did not lie in the political arguments of the élite. In 1830 the liberals were afraid of a re-run of the 1790s, and indeed were only held together as a loose political group by their opposition to the Polignac government. In 1848 the banquet campaign had no cohesion. The actual overthrow of the established regime was in both cases the product of the coincidence of heightened political debate with two other circumstances, the social impact of economic depression and the absence of adequate physical force and government confidence to control central Paris.

Artisan revolution

On both occasions the actual revolutions were the work of the artisans of central Paris. Paris was the fastest-growing industrial area in France. Its population almost doubled to one million in the first half of the nineteenth century through migration of workers from rural areas. Parisian industry was particularly vulnerable to violent fluctuations in these years because of the emphasis on luxury goods, metalwork, cabinet-making and the building trades. Relatively rapid industrial growth in these years alternated with prolonged financial crises when confidence collapsed, accompanied by commercial and industrial setbacks. The resulting short-time working and unemployment was made much worse and more prolonged when such problems were also linked to harvest failure. This occurred in both 1827–32 and 1845–48. Artisans had to cope with accelerating food costs (50% +) at a time when work was scarce. Food shortages and setbacks in rural industry encouraged more people to migrate to the larger towns, especially the capital. It has been estimated that perhaps 10,000 artisans were unemployed in Paris on the eve of the February Revolution 1848.

Artisans responded by trying to put pressure on local and central government. They wanted merchants and employers to pay a living rate, the government to abandon legislation which protected producers by keeping out foreign grain until French grain prices made bread a luxury, to abolish or reform indirect taxes like those on wine and to provide adequate temporary unemployment pay. Marches and demonstrations were commonplace in these years of dearth and industrial setback. From both 1827 to beyond 1832 and 1845 to 1848, Paris was the centre of repeated worker protests. Bread, grain and wine tax riots and scattered industrial disputes became common throughout France, but in Paris prolonged economic crises threatened serious political destabilisation.

Parisian geography was to blame. Unlike England, where rapid industrialisation with its consequent problems was far distant from the centre of government, in France the two existed in the same districts of the capital. What made France volatile was the geographical accident which located a highly-centralised political system, a lively newspaper press and a vocal and politicised artisanate in the same streets between the Tuileries and the Hotel-de-Ville on the right bank of the Seine. In 1830 liberal deputies cringed in their fine mansions as artisan demonstrations swept through their own streets. When the Ordinances of St Cloud threatened the liberal press, the discontented workers left their workplace to join crowds of artisans in the same streets. Thus the three elements which constituted demonstrations and revolution in these years were intimate neighbours. A sufficiently large and determined riot could topple the very centralised political framework. Why?

A revolutionary army?

In both 1830 and 1848 the established system was overcome far more by its own inadequacy than by the force of any opponent. Numbers and attitude were crucial. In 1830 there were simply too few soldiers available (about 6,000) to control the city. Military planning was disastrously negligent. No arrangements were made to rest and feed the troops. The National Guard, which might have provided an alternative force for law and order, had been disbanded by the King in 1827 on suspicion of disloyalty. Members were quick to appear in the Three Glorious Days of July 1830 in full uniform, but in support of the rebels not the King. A similar story could be told of 1848, when national guardsmen showed more sympathy for a republic than the Citizen-King. Attitude counted for a good deal. On neither occasion did either King try to resist dismissal. In 1830 the ultra-royalists and the liberals alike were terrified of the spectre of revolutionary upheaval, as indeed were those who had benefited from the July Days of 1830 during the events of February 1848.

The legacy of 1789 was a tradition of political instability, not inevitable social revolution. 1830 was bourgeois only in that it confirmed the dominance of an élite. There was a notable absence of social conflict within the wealthier groups in 1848. It was the rapid industrialisation of Paris, with recurring recessions and harvest setbacks, which provided the shock troops of revolution, a revolution much feared by the wealthy and quite unprofitable for the poor.

Further Reading

Collingham, H.A.C. *The July Monarchy: A Political History of France 1830–48* (Longman, 1988).
Fortescue, W. *Revolution and Counter-Revolution in France 1815–52* (Historical Association Studies, Blackwell, 1988).
Jardin, A. and Tudesq, A.J. *Restoration and Reaction 1815–48* (Cambridge University Press, 1983).
Magraw, R. *France 1815–1914: The Bourgeois Century* (Fontana, 1983).
Pinkney, D.H. *The French Revolution of 1830* (Princeton, 1972).
Pinkney, D.H. *Decisive Years in France 1840–47* (Princeton, 1986).
Roberts, J. *The Counter-Revolution in France 1789–1830* (Macmillan, 1990).
Sewell, W. *Work and Revolution in France: The Language of Labour from the Old Regime to 1848* (Cambridge, 1980).

Pamela Pilbeam is Reader in Modern European History at Royal Holloway and Bedford New College, University of London. She is author of *The 1830 Revolution in France* (Macmillan, 1991) and *The Middle Classes in Europe 1789–1914: France, Germany, Italy and Russia* (Macmillan, 1990).

David Saunders
Alexander I of Russia: Reformer or Reactionary?

Schizophrenic, poseur, or committed reformer? A portrait of the tsar who ruled Russia at the time of the Napoleonic Wars.

Historians often explain the kaleidoscopic policies of Alexander I by pointing to his genes, his upbringing, and the manner of his accession. Whereas his grandmother, Catherine the Great, was one of the most philosophically-inclined rulers of eighteenth-century Europe, his father, Paul, was obsessed with soldiers. Whereas Catherine subjected him as a child to the enlightened opinions of the Swiss republican Frédéric-César de La Harpe, Paul enticed him with war-games. The conspiracy which brought him to the throne in March 1801 had his blessing, but the murder of his father left him with a lifelong sense of guilt. So, the argument runs, inconsistency was inevitable. Sometimes Alexander behaved like Catherine, sometimes he behaved like Paul.

But the tsar's changes of tack can also be explained by pointing to the problems he had to deal with. The intractability of the Russian Empire gave him every reason for periodic faintheartedness. The demands of war and diplomacy distracted him continually. If the emphasis is placed on these material difficulties, the remarkable thing about Alexander turns out to be not inconsistency but the determination and frequency with which he returned to the path of reform. Very few tsars remained so hopeful for so long.

An intractable empire

The Russian Empire in 1801 posed daunting problems. Its soil was infertile, its climate bleak. The vast majority of its inhabitants were peasants. It was ethnically diverse. No more than 70,000 pupils were receiving instruction in a population of some 41 million; no more than 6.9% of the inhabitants of the European part of the empire aged ten and over were literate. The budget was in chaos. The state's outgoings exceeded its revenue by an average of a third in the first ten years of the nineteenth century. Paper money and the debasement of the coinage generated rampant inflation. Civil servants were in short supply. In answer to the question how Russia's bureaucracy 'managed to govern so many people and so much territory', Robert Jones says of the later eighteenth century 'that for the most part it could not and did not govern them'. Catherine the Great's provincial reform of 1775 had entailed the winding-down of the central administrative machinery set up by Peter the Great some 60 years previously. Only the nobility appeared to be prospering, but by 1800 even nobles were beginning to experience a crisis of confidence because of the gradual emergence of the very bureaucrats who were not yet numerous enough to replace them.

Reform (1801–5)

Alexander addressed himself to these difficulties within months of ascending the throne. Gathering a few close friends around him, he engaged in wide-ranging discussion of plans for reform. Significant changes resulted. The creation of the State Council in 1801 and of central government ministries in September 1802 offered the chance of greater efficiency in the upper levels of the imperial administration. An edict of 1803 made it theoretically possible for serfs to own land. Statutes of 1803 and 1804 introduced a four-tier system of education which looked considerably more sophisticated than that created by Catherine the Great's Statute on Popular Schools of 1786. Edicts of 1804 marked the beginning of serf emancipation in the Baltic provinces and an improvement in the circumstances of the empire's Jews. The tsar's dream of codifying Russian law came to nothing, but his reformism set in train a hunt for guiding principles which his successors were never to arrest. The poet Pushkin was to speak of 'the beautiful beginning of Alexander's days.'

War (1805–7)

Then war intervened. Alexander had come to terms with France almost immediately after ascending the throne, but from the second half of 1803 it became increasingly evident that he would have to return to the fray. Napoleon had been interfering openly in the affairs of northern Italy, Switzerland, and Holland, and had presided over changes in the Holy Roman Empire which undermined the position of the Habsburgs without enhancing the role of Prussia. One way or another, most of the European land mass seemed to be in French hands. In a fulminating speech at the State Council in April 1804 the tsar's friend, Adam Czartoryski, argued that Napoleon's abduction and execution of the Duc d'Enghien warranted the wrath of the whole of the continent. Russia entered into negotiations with Britain. In 1805 the two countries committed themselves to 'The establishment of a European order which effectively guarantees the safety and independence of the different States and constitutes a firm barrier against future encroachments.' Austria and Prussia associated themselves with the Anglo-Russian alliance and armies took the field.

Britain won the battle of Trafalgar, but Austria withdrew from the war after Austerlitz (December 1805), Prussia after Jena (October 1806), and Russia after Friedland (June 1807). At the Tilsit negotiations which followed the battle of Friedland, Alexander had little option but to accept France's offer of an alliance. Napoleon obliged him to participate in France's scheme to throttle Britain's trade by closing mainland Europe to British ships.

The effect on the Russian economy of involvement in this 'Continental System' was highly detrimental. British ships had carried 63% of the goods exported from St Petersburg in 1804. Without their involvement as carriers, Russia could neither buy nor sell to the desired extent. France was in no position to replace Britian as Russia's main trading partner. France could not supply the goods Russia needed, had no use for many of the staple Russian exports, and could not trade by sea. Without British goods and British ships, the Russian economy became ever more parochial. Meanwhile, Napoleon obliged Alexander to launch an attack on Sweden and urged him to prosecute more vigorously a war with the Ottoman Empire into which he had been drawn in 1806. The Grand Duchess Catherine, sister of the tsar, became a rallying point in St Petersburg for the many Russian critics of Alexander's diplomatic realignment.

Reform (1807–12)

It was remarkable, in these circumstances, that Alexander gave Mikhail Speranskii the chance to return to the path of domestic reform. How this son of a provincial priest penetrated the highest levels of the imperial bureaucracy is the stuff of novels. By 1807 he had risen high enough to be appointed Deputy Minister of Justice and State Secretary. From late 1808 until early 1812 he was the most powerful Russian below the throne.

Historians have only recently begun to present Speranskii convincingly. Marc Raeff's influential biography, first published in 1957, depicts him as an open-minded conservative. The publication of the statesman's papers in 1961 made possible a different view, but Raeff failed to take proper account of them when the second edition of his book came out in 1969. In an early memorandum Speranskii listed the characteristics of his ideal constitution. They included the participation of free social elements in the making of laws, the power of public opinion to prevent the law from being implemented perversely, the responsibility of the executive to 'an independent social layer', a system of civil and criminal law acceptable to the community, an independent judiciary, open government, the freedom of the press, 'an adequate level of education and an abundance of the means needed to execute the laws'. In the context of the early ninteenth-century Russian Empire, a person who pursued objectives like these was a red-hot radical.

Speranskii had no intention of keeping his ideas to himself. In late 1809 he proposed giving the State Council general oversight of a revamped imperial administration in which the legislative, executive, and judicial arms of the government would be clearly separated from each other. The legislative arm was to consist of a four-tier system of representative assemblies stretching from the canton level at the bottom to a State Duma or parliament at the top. Raeff conveys the impression that the purpose of these proposals was only to make the Russian autocracy run more efficiently, but Speranskii stated unequivocally that the foundations of the autocracy were to change: it was 'essential to allow the participation of the people in the making of law'. The State Secretary was less insistent on the need to transform the Russian Empire's social structure, but 'There is no justification for supposing,' he wrote, 'that [civil slavery] cannot be abolished in Russia, provided effective measures are taken to this end'.

Some of Speranskii's ideas reached the statute book. In 1809 he secured the enactment of a law which imposed examinations on officials who sought to rise in the civil service. After Russia took Finland from Sweden (in the war which resulted from Alexander's alliance with France), Speranskii devised far more generous constitutional arrangements for the newly-acquired Grand Duchy than those which were obtained in the empire at large. A reorganised State Council started functioning on 1 January 1810. Statutes of July 1810 and June 1811 clarified some of the demarcation lines within and between the ministries of 1802. Edicts of 1810 and 1812 threatened to end the nobility's longstanding immunity from direct taxation. In May 1810 the government announced its intention of making state lands available for sale to all 'free classes' rather than just the traditional landowners. The Imperial Lycée founded at Tsarskoe Selo on Speranskii's suggestion in 1811 soon became one of the outstanding educational institutions of the empire. The Committee of Ministers which had been introduced in 1802 was put on a sounder footing in 1812.

Many of these changes had flaws, and much remained undone. The adjustments in the procedure of the Committee of Ministers did not imply the introduction of cabinet government. The effect of partial rather than wholesale implementation of the purely administrative aspects of Speranskii's proposals was to complicate the state machine rather than streamline it. The measures which tended in the direction of equalising taxation met with the tsar's approval solely on grounds of financial necessity. Speranskii expended a great deal of energy on a scheme to divide the Senate into executive and judicial halves, but Alexander let it fall by the wayside. The State Secretary's advocacy of local assemblies and a central Duma or parliament came to nothing. The notion of promoting social fluidity went by the board virtually completely.

If the alliance with France had remained stable, however, Speranskii might have corrected his mistakes and striven to complete his programme. Although the Grand Duchess Catherine orchestrated a campaign against him by commissioning and submitting to Alexander a reactionary diatribe from the pen of the historian Nikolai Karamzin, international relations rather than domestic opposition put paid to the reformer's career. In 1812 Alexander was compelled by events beyond his control to retreat from change. He dismissed Speranskii in order to give his undivided attention to the renewal of the war.

War (1812–15)

Russia withdrew from the 'Continental System' when its economic effects became intolerable. Napoleon tried to force Russia to rejoin by invading, but failed to procure a decisive military engagement. The French occupation of Moscow turned out to be a Pyrrhic victory. By the time what was left of the *Grande Armée* withdrew across the River Niemen at the end of 1812, the capacity of France to challenge the Russian Empire had been exhausted.

Russia, however, was exhausted too. Alexander ought to have listened to those in his entourage who advised him to give up chasing the French at the frontier. Instead, he made the biggest mistake of his reign. By taking his forces into central and western Europe he saddled himself, eventually, with a permanent part in policing the continent. He compounded the error at the Congress of Vienna in 1815. Although Russia sought only the annexation of Napoleon's Grand Duchy of Warsaw, the tsar gave the other participants in the Congress the impression that, after annexation, he intended to engage in additional forward moves. Britain, Austria, and a rehabilitated France formed an alliance against him in January 1815 which threatened to put paid to the peacemaking. Alexander compromised and eventually received almost as much Polish territory as he would have done anyway, but he had succeeded in engendering an atmosphere of mistrust which augured ill for the future of Russian diplomacy.

Reform (1815–20)

At home, however, Alexander turned once again to reform. Because, after 1812, he lent an increasingly receptive ear to religious mystics, and because he permitted the blinkered artillery officer Aleksei Arakcheev to succeed Speranskii as his right-hand man in domestic affairs, he led contemporaries (and a number of historians) to suppose that he was descending into obscurantism. The impression was unfortunate but misleading. Even the tsar's disasters sprang from good intentions. His Bible Society fell prey to bigots, but when he brought it into being at the end of 1812 he hoped that it would shed light in dark places. Arakcheev turned the 'military colonies' into a primary focus of social resentment, but at the point they became a major plank of the government's programme (in 1815), the idea behind them was to create an environment in which soldiers could flourish in peacetime.

Other post-war measures need no explaining away. On converting Napoleon's Grand Duchy of Warsaw into a Russian-ruled Kingdom of Poland, Alexander granted it one of the most progressive political systems in Europe. In a speech at the first session of the Polish parliament in March 1818 he hinted that one day he would extend 'liberal institutions' to all the territories in his charge. Then he ordered his close associate Nikolai Novosil'tsev to draw up a pan-imperial constitutional charter. The document spoke of decentralisation, civil liberties, and a range of elective assemblies. It did not become law, but it was more than a pipe-dream. In October 1819, Alexander approved what was probably the final version. When, early the following month, he created a new governor-generalship out of a group of provinces south of Moscow and sent a top St Petersburg bureaucrat to run it, he may have been taking a tentative step in the direction of the charter's idea of decentralised vicegerencies.

Since, in the years immediately after the end of the war, Alexander also emancipated the serfs of the empire's Baltic provinces, abolished mutilation as a judicial penalty, made liberal constitutional arrangements for the recently acquired province of Bessarabia, and instructed Arakcheev to try and find a way of emancipating the serfs of the imperial heartland, he was clearly far from abandoning the liberal impulses with which he had ascended the throne in 1801.

Disillusion (1820–5)

It is true that Alexander shifted to the right around 1820, but his reasons for doing so were the same as those which had tied his hands from the start: the intractability of the empire and events abroad. The war had exacerbated strains in the countryside. Land-lords who had suffered financially felt the need to press their serfs harder. Peasants who had fought in the militia or as partisans were reluctant to return to their servile condition. Peasant cottage indus-try had received a fillip from the damage which the French invasion had done to Russian factories. More peasants were engaging in trade. To protect their gains, an increasing number of peasants took the technically illegal step of submitting petitions to the tsar. More of them took up arms. Their disturbances went on longer. Of the 150 instances in which troops had to be called out against serfs in Alexander's reign, 66 took place between 1816 and 1820. In 1820 the biggest rural disturbance of the first quarter of the nineteenth century came to a head on the River Don. After General Chernyshev put it down, the tsar closed the door on reform in the countryside.

In foreign affairs Alexander's room for idealism diminished very soon after the Congress of Vienna. German students gave him serious cause for concern in October 1817 by demonstrating at the Wartburg Castle near Eisenach to mark the 300th anniversary of the Reformation. For a while Alexander hoped that censorship and strict control of the universities would be enough to prevent the recurrence of such incidents, but Metternich, the Chancellor of the Austrian Empire, eventually persuaded him to change his mind. When, in March 1819, the German student Karl Sand murdered the right-wing playwright August von Kotzebue at Mannheim, Metter-nich decided on a crackdown. His 'Karlsbad Decrees' of October 1819 were the prelude to furious international wrangling about the extent and nature of the Great Powers' responsibility for the European status quo. After the murder of a member of the French ruling house, an uprising in Spain, the collapse of the Kingdom of the Two Sicilies, and especially the mutiny in October 1820 of a guards regiment in St Petersburg, Alexander came to believe that only strong-arm tactics could prevent the outbreak of pan-European revolution. When Austrian troops crossed into Italy at the beginning of 1821, he gave them his blessing. In 1822 he ordered the suppres-sion of Russian freemasonry. In 1823, he waxed enthusiastic about French intervention in Spain. By the time of his death in November 1825 he had identified himself almost wholly with the forces of order.

Conclusion

Thus the last five years of Alexander's reign were inglorious. The uprising which followed his death – the 'first Russian Revolution' of December 1825 – arose partly out of the frustration felt by educated contemporaries at what they thought was the tsar's lack of interest in his own reform agenda. Yet Alexander had spent longer reforming than fighting or backsliding. In view of his frequent returns to the path of change and the size of the problems he was trying to solve, it is wiser, on balance, to applaud his radicalism than to accuse him of superficiality or window-dressing.

Further Reading

Grimsted, P.K. *The Foreign Ministers of Alexander I* (University of California Press, 1969).

Jenkins, M. *Arakcheev* (Faber and Faber, 1969).

Jones, R.E. *Provincial Development in Russia* (Rutgers University Press, 1984).

McConnell, A. *Tsar Alexander I* (AHM Publishing Company, 1970).

Mazour, A.G. *The First Russian Revolution, 1825* (Stanford University Press, 1937, repr. 1964).

Palmer, A. *Alexander I* (Weidenfeld and Nicolson, 1974).

Pipes, R. *Russia Observed* (Westview Press, 1989).

Raeff, M. *Michael Speransky* (Martinus Nijhoff, 1957, 2nd edn 1969).

Saunders, D. *Russia in the Age of Reaction and Reform 1801–81* (Longman, 1992).

Zawadzki, W.H. *A Man of Honour: Adam Czartoryski as a Statesman of Russia and Poland 1795–1831* (Oxford University Press, 1993).

David Saunders is Senior Lecturer in History at the University of Newcastle upon Tyne.

William Fortescue
Europe in Revolt:
The 1848 Revolutions

Why did revolutions occur across most of Europe in 1848? And why, in most places, were Ancien Régimes able to reassert themselves?

The revolutionary movements in Europe during 1848 and 1849 universally failed in their short-term objectives, yet nevertheless were of enormous importance. They helped to ensure that a conservative social and political order was maintained and consolidated in Europe until the First World War; that the national unifications of Germany and Italy were achieved within a conservative framework; that violent revolutionary movements (though not, of course, anarchism and terrorism) virtually disappeared in Europe until the First World War, the only significant exceptions being the Paris Commune of 1871 and the Russian Revolution of 1905–6, both of which occurred only after catastrophic military defeats; and that it required the cataclysm of the First World War before Europe experienced a new wave of revolutionary upheaval.

Economic crisis

One of the fundamental causes of the revolutions of 1848 was an economic crisis. This crisis was principally due to failures in the cereal and potato harvests throughout most of Europe in 1845 and 1846. Poor communications, the generally inadequate response of political authorities, panic buying by consumers and speculation by merchants accentuated the impact of these harvest failures. As a result, the basic foodstuffs of the poor, for whom food was the major item in the household budget, became scarce and expensive. This, in turn, led to a sharp reduction in consumer spending on items other than foodstuffs. Consequently, craft and industrial production suffered a steep fall in demand, to which merchants and employers responded by cancelling orders and laying off workers. Therefore, from 1847 onwards unemployment rapidly increased. At the same time, a financial crisis, made worse by a speculative boom in the early 1840s, developed, manifesting itself in a sudden rise in bankruptcies, crippling levels of indebtedness for many industrial and agricultural producers, a drying up of investment capital, and a rapid decline in all construction work. All this helped to prolong the economic crisis for some years after harvests had returned to average levels of production, so that most of Europe did not experience full economic recovery until the early 1850s.

A number of observations can be made about this economic crisis. The main initial cause of the economic crisis was cereal and potato harvest failures, which indicates the extent to which agriculture still dominated the European economy. Only in Britain and Belgium were urbanisation and industrialisation really important by 1848, and, significantly, they remained relatively immune from the revolutionary movements of 1848 and 1849. The increase in Europe's population since 1815 aggravated the impact of the economic crisis. Most rural areas of Europe were more populous by the mid-nineteenth century than ever before, and urban populations had tended to increase even more dramatically, so that the populations of cities such as Paris and Berlin approximately doubled between 1815 and 1848. Because of the continuing dominance of agriculture in the European economy, and because of the limited role before 1848 of such modernising factors as new technology, factory production, railways and banks, this expanded population was highly vulnerable to agricultural crises.

Governments everywhere in Europe failed to intervene effectively to alleviate the social distress and reverse the economic collapse produced by the crisis, partly because they lacked the will due to an adherence to *laissez-faire* economic principles, partly because they lacked the means due to an absence of adequate financial and bureaucratic resources. Therefore, governments and regimes became discredited amongst the rural and urban masses, who were generally excluded from direct participation in national politics and who might have little concern for political issues such as court scandals, constitutional reform or foreign policy, but who could be politicised by a major economic failure.

The harvests of 1847 were reasonably good, as were the harvests of the following years. Consequently, governments and ruling classes tended to assume that the worst of the economic crisis was over by the winter of 1847–8, which helps to explain why the revolutionary explosions of January, February and March 1848 took them by surprise. After the autumn of 1847 food became relatively cheap and plentiful, except when political and military developments interrupted distribution. Peasants and farmers now had to cope with relatively low agricultural prices, and even overproduction in the case of wine, but they were not generally faced with economic ruin, unless they were wholly engaged in the production of a cash crop such as cork, olives, hemp or flax, for which the demand had drastically declined, or in the production of silk, which continued to experience poor harvests from 1848 to 1851. Hence the rural populations of Europe were not generally in a desperate economic situation in 1848 and 1849, which helps to explain their relatively unenthusiastic support for revolutionary movements, and even their role in suppressing revolutionary movements, by voting for conservative candidates in elections (particularly in France) and by serving as military conscripts virtually everywhere. In contrast, for the urban poor the economic situation generally deteriorated in 1847 and 1848, so that they suffered exceptionally high levels of unemployment and were often ready recruits for revolutionary movements.

Finally, the very difficult economic and financial situation in Europe in 1848 and 1849 handicapped governments and regimes of all political complexions. State treasuries were exhausted. Yet demands for state expenditure were exceptionally high, to alleviate social distress, to promote economic recovery and to finance military operations; and governments had little room for financial manoeuvre: the sale of public assets was not usually a viable option (an exception being the confiscation and redistribution of Church property by the Roman Republic in 1849), loans could not be raised easily, and political pressures called for taxes to be reduced, not increased.

Political crisis

The retention of political power throughout Europe by conservative, if not reactionary, regimes, which favoured the interests of small, privileged and disproportionately wealthy élites, could always provoke opposition, especially when a severe economic crisis made the incompetence of governments and the inequitable distribution of wealth especially hard to tolerate. In addition, certain monarchs and ministers, such as King Louis Philippe and Guizot in France, Metternich in the Habsburg Empire and King Ludwig in Bavaria, had attracted an exceptional degree of personal unpopularity; and manifestations of liberalism and of movements for constitutional reform occurred throughout Europe in 1846 and 1847: Chartism in Britain, the amnesties and reform of Pope Pius IX, the liberal victory in the Baden parliamentary election of 1846, the special parliament summoned by the Kings of Württemberg, Prussia and Saxony, the reform banquet campaign in France, the Sonderbund struggle in Switzerland and the demonstrations of opposition to Habsburg rule in Lombardy, Venetia and Hungary. These political factors interacted with the economic crisis through facilitating the emergence of broad opposition fronts of liberal nobles, bourgeois professionals, urban workers and peasant farmers against those in power.

The revolt in Palermo against Bourbon rule in Sicily in January 1848 might have been an isolated event but for the overthrow of

Louis Philippe and the proclamation of the Second Republic in France on 24 February 1848. This represented a traumatic blow to the 1815 Settlement in one of Europe's most important states, and suggested that revolutionary change could apparently be achieved relatively easily. In an obvious chain reaction, popular demonstrations in Vienna forced the resignation of Metternich (13 March); the Austrian garrison in Venice was compelled to withdraw and a Venetian republic was proclaimed (17 March); an Austrian garrison was similarly expelled from Milan (18 March); and King Frederick William IV of Prussia ordered his troops to leave Berlin (19 March). Elsewhere, revolutionary and nationalist movements challenged the survival of the German States and of the Habsburg Empire.

A common pattern of events can be discerned. Massive antiregime demonstrations occurred in capital cities such as Palermo, Paris, Vienna, Buda-Pest, Venice, Milan and Berlin. Regimes capitulated because those in power were too panicked to respond effectively and because soldiers and police were unable or unwilling to clear the streets. Therefore, concessions were immediately granted: the withdrawal of troops, the appointment of new liberal governments, the granting or promising of liberal and constitutional reforms, the formation of civil militias or national guards. However, these revolutions were essentially rapid transfers of power or, in the case of Hungary, the creation of a partial power vacuum. Only two monarchs lost their thrones, Louis Philippe in France and Ludwig in Bavaria; and Ludwig was succeeded by his son, Maximilian II. Later, on 2 December 1848, Emperor Ferdinand I of Austria abdicated in favour of his nephew, Francis Joseph, but as part of a reassertion of conservative Habsburg authority. Above all, state bureaucracies, professional armies and social hierarchies more or less survived the upheavals of the Spring of 1848.

France and the German States

In France the moderate republicans lost the political initiative and were succeeded within a year by Louis Napoleon Bonaparte, Napoleon's nephew and political heir. The Provisional government, which immediately replaced Louis Philippe and Guizot, had a moderate republican majority and introduced quite a remarkable political programme, including the proclamation of the Second Republic, the introduction of manhood suffrage and the abolition of slavery in France's colonies. However, the continuing economic crisis was blamed on the Provisional government, which, in addition, alienated the traditional ruling classes by its apparent radicalism and willingness to appease the Left, the peasantry by its massive 45% increase of the property tax (the 45 centime tax), and the urban poor, particularly of Paris, by its failure to introduce radical measures and to combat unemployment. After conservatives had won a large majority in the National Assembly elections of 23 April 1848, a clash between the conservative parliament and the Parisian working class was probably inevitable. It came on 24 June 1848, when the virtual closure of the unemployment relief scheme offered by the National Workshops sparked off a popular insurrection. The suppression of this popular insurrection by the army and National Guard was accompanied by the transfer of executive powers to General Cavaignac and by a further erosion of the position of the moderate republicans. During the summer and autumn of 1848 a new popular conservatism developed, linking the defence of order, property, religion and the family to the mystique of Bonapartism; and, after the National Assembly had decided that the entire electorate should directly choose a president vested with executive powers, a massive popular vote swept Louis Napoleon Bonaparte to presidential power on 10 December 1848.

The February 1848 Revolution in France, and the subsequent fall of Metternich, had a profound impact on the German States. They were suddenly confronted with fears of a French invasion, serious outbreaks of urban riots and peasant disorders, and a confident opposition demanding the dismissal of reactionary ministers, the introduction of liberal reforms, and the holding of national and state parliamentary elections on the basis of manhood suffrage. However, the French invasion did not materialise, and concessions and reforms, together with some repression (particularly in Baden), contained the political violence. In addition, the election of a German national parliament produced in the Frankfurt parliament a less revolutionary assembly than might have been expected; and the Frankfurt parliament immediately faced a series of crises beyond its capabilities, since it had no financial resources, no bureaucracy and no army. Voters had to be economically independent and citizens of the state in which they voted, which disenfranchised both the poor and migrant workers, while those elected tended to be university-educated members of the professional middle classes, who were not representative of the German population as a whole. The elections themselves alienated non-German ethnic minorities, such as the Poles in Posen, the Italians in the South Tirol, the Czechs in Bohemia, and the Slovenes in other parts of the Habsburg Empire. The development of a Polish revolt in Posen, and the opening of a Slav Congress in Prague (2 June 1848), provided Prussian and Habsburg armies respectively with the opportunity to win easy victories. In contrast, at the Treaty of Malmo (26 August 1848) Prussia abandoned attempts to gain military control of the Duchies of Schleswig and Holstein in return for an armistice with

Denmark, the lifting of a Danish naval blockade, and the right to share with Denmark the nomination of the common administration of the two Duchies. After stormy debates and violent demonstrations, the Frankfurt parliament reluctantly accepted the Malmo Treaty (16 September 1848), which many Germans regarded as a national humiliation. Meanwhile, the liberal-conservative majority in the Frankfurt parliament failed both to tackle social and economic grievances and to establish a constitutional monarchy, headed either by a Habsburg prince, the Archduke John of Austria (the choice of most South German Catholics), or by King Frederick William IV of Prussia (the choice of most North German Protestants). Thus, as Prussian troops suppressed the last remnants of the revolutionary and nationalist movement in Germany, the Frankfurt parliament disintegrated during May and June 1849.

The Habsburg Empire

The main challenge to the Habsburg Empire came from the Czech rising in Prague, the revolutionary movement in Vienna, and the nationalist revolts in Lombardy, Venetia and Hungary. In Prague, the Habsburg army commander, Windischgratz, exploited Czech student disturbances on 12 June 1848 as a pretext for a military occupation of the Bohemian capital. It was an easy Habsburg victory, since the Czechs were taken by surprise and lacked military organisation and leadership, and Prague then had a significant German-speaking community which sided with the Habsburgs. In Vienna, the revolutionary movement tended to split into its component elements of moderate liberals seeking liberal reforms and constitutional government, radical students who wanted to destroy the Habsburg Empire, and urban workers demanding employment and welfare. The flight of the Emperor and his Court to Innsbruck in May 1848 deprived the Viennese revolutionaries of a valuable asset. Also, Vienna remained isolated from the rest of the Habsburg Empire, particularly as the progressive dismantling of the feudal system, climaxing with the abolition of forced peasant labour by the Emancipation Act of 7 September 1848, confirmed the acceptance of Habsburg rule by the Austrian peasantry. On 6 October 1848, violent resistance in Vienna to the despatch of troops to put down the Magyar rising did lead to a major insurrection, but this was overcome by regular troops under Windischgratz.

Immediately after the successful revolts in Milan and Venice, the restoration of Habsburg rule in Lombardy and Venetia must have seemed unlikely. Yet the Habsburg forces were not destroyed, but allowed to regroup in the fortified Italian cities known as the Quadrilateral (Verona, Mantua, Legnago and Peschiera); and the

Lombard rebels and Daniele Manin, leader of the Venetian Republic, failed to develop effective military forces of their own or to secure decisive outside assistance. Pope Pius IX on 29 April 1848 condemned the anti-Habsburg revolts in Northern Italy, a condemnation which inevitably had considerable influence, particularly for the Catholic clergy and the peasantry. Amongst other states, the French Second Republic, the Kingdom of the Two Sicilies and Piedmont provided little more than token aid to Venice, while Britain remained hostile. Only King Charles Albert of Piedmont rallied to the Milanese. However, this turned the Lombard revolt into an Austrian-Piedmontese war which aroused the patriotism of many German-Austrians; Charles Albert as a monarch with territorial ambitions constituted an unlikely saviour of a republican revolt; and in any case his two invasions of Lombardy were successfully checked by his defeats at Custoza (25 July 1848) and Novara (23 March 1849). Venice held out till 22 August 1849, but the prolonged resistance, while heroic, was doomed to failure, given Habsburg control of the sea and of the hinterland.

In Hungary the long power vacuum, which began when Habsburg rule became ineffective in March 1848, allowed Kossuth to establish a Magyar state. Kossuth and the Hungarian Diet achieved much, including liberal reforms, the abolition of feudalism and the creation of an Hungarian army. The emphasis, though, on the Magyar language alienated ethnic minorities such as the Rumanians, Slovaks, Germans, Croats, Serbs and Ukranians, as did Hungarian claims on Slovenia, Croatia, Transylvania and the Military Border. This inevitably produced a reaction against the Magyars, who constituted less than half of Hungary's population. From July 1848 Jellacic organised Croatia as a separate province and in September invaded Hungary at the head of a Croatian army. The Vienna insurrection in October 1848 diverted Habsburg forces to the imperial capital, but the Magyars failed to link up with this insurrection. With Vienna recaptured and other territories coming under Habsburg control, the subduing of the isolated Magyar revolt could begin. Only in April 1849, emboldened by Hungarian military successes, did Kossuth finally proclaim the Habsburg dynasty to be deposed and Hungary to be completely independent. This proclamation, and further Habsburg reverses, forced the Habsburgs on 1 May 1849 to request Russian military assistance, which finally sealed the fate of the Magyar revolt.

The Papal States and the Kingdom of the Two Sicilies

The story of Hungary was to some extent repeated in the Papal States. The power vacuum following the assassination of Count

Rossi (15 November 1848) and the flight of Pius IX (25 November 1848) enabled a Roman Republic to emerge under the leadership of Mazzini and Garibaldi. The Roman Republic brought liberal reforms, a public works programme and an elected parliament, but it remained isolated, with even Tuscany refusing to support it. Despite the valiant efforts of Garibaldi and the army which he created and commanded, the Roman Republic was overwhelmed, and Pius IX restored, by foreign military intervention – mainly French, but also Spanish, Habsburg and Neapolitan – between April and July 1849.

The risings in the Kingdom of the Two Sicilies remained isolated from events elsewhere, but they conformed to a familiar pattern. After the initial shock administered by a wave of urban riots and peasant brigandage, the Bourbon regime reasserted itself, while liberals and property-owners abandoned their revolutionary enthusiasm when order, property and economic recovery seemed to be threatened. The attempt by the Sicilian Parliament to establish an independent Sicily was opposed by the traditional ruling class and not supported by the peasantry. In addition, the Sicilian parliament both refused Bourbon offers of Sicilian autonomy and failed to create an effective army, so that, after a six-month armistice imposed by the British and French in September 1848 had expired, a Bourbon army re-entered Palermo virtually unopposed. In Naples, the re-establishment of royal authority followed an unsuccessful popular insurrection on 15 May 1848.

Conclusions

The failure of the majority of the peasantry to support the revolutionary and nationalist movements of 1848 and 1849 was of crucial importance. Of course, peasants were not necessarily or universally conservative. In France significant peasant radicalism is evident in the National Assembly elections of May 1849 and in the resistance to Louis Napoleon Bonaparte's *coup d'état* of December 1851. Sporadic peasant violence occurred in the German States, but could be contained without serious difficulty, except in Posen. The Kingdom of the Two Sicilies experienced peasant brigandage, though this could be as much criminal as revolutionary activity. Nevertheless, in general the European peasantry remained indifferent, or hostile, to the revolutionary and nationalist movements, except in Hungary and the Roman Republic. Another widespread phenomenon was the collapse of united opposition fronts, as the different opposition elements separated from each other, and as fears for family, order, religion, property and economic recovery encouraged support for traditional authorities. Finally, the old regime triumphed everywhere with the assistance of effective political and military leadership and of professional armies, while capable revolutionary armies were not created, again except in Hungary and the Roman Republic.

The revolutionary and nationalist movements in Europe of 1848 and 1849 were arguably, though, only a partial failure. Some of the achievements of those years were irreversible, such as the abolition of the remnants of feudalism, the introduction of manhood suffrage in France and the general impetus to democracy and parliamentary government. Also, an important stimulus had been given to the development of a national political consciousness in many states. Equally, the upheavals of 1848 and 1849, and the brutal way in which they were suppressed, ensured that such issues as republicanism in France, the unifications of Italy and Germany, and the separation of Hungary and Bohemia from Austria, remained on Europe's political agenda.

Further Reading

Langer, W.L. *Political and Social Upheaval, 1832–52* (Harper and Row, 1969).

Price, R. *The Revolutions of 1848* (Macmillan, 1988).

Roberts, I.W. *Nicholas I and the Russian Intervention in Hungary* (Macmillan, 1991).

Sperber, J. *Rhineland Radicals: the Democratic Movement and the Revolution of 1848–49* (Princeton, 1991).

William Fortescue is Lecturer in History at the University of Kent at Canterbury. He is the author of *Alphonse de Lamartine, a Political Biography* (1983) and *Revolution and Counter-Revolution in France, 1815–52* (1988).

David Moon
The Serfs' Perspective on Emancipation

David Moon examines the difficulty of explaining emancipation to the serfs and the confused hopes and aspirations which this gave rise to.

Most textbooks on Russian history and many of the more specialised studies have approached the abolition of serfdom in Russia from the points of view of Tsar Alexander II, the imperial bureaucracy and the landed nobility. The purpose of this article is to look at abolition from the perspective of the people it most directly affected: the 22 million Russian serfs. The article starts by considering the serfs' status on the eve of 1861. This is necessary in order to understand how serfs were affected by the terms of abolition, which is discussed in the second part of the article. The final part focuses on the immediate reactions by former serfs to abolition, paying particular attention to how, or indeed whether, they understood the reform.

The serfs' status

Serfs comprised slightly under half the peasant population of Russia on the eve of abolition. Most Russian peasants were small-scale subsistence farmers who relied on the labour of their families to cultivate small plots of land. Unlike 'capitalist' farmers, they did not aim to produce a large harvest to sell at a profit at the market. Instead, they endeavoured to produce sufficient to support their families, and a surplus to sell to raise some money. They used this money to buy the few essentials they could not produce themselves, and to pay the dues and taxes demanded from them by the outside world. Many peasants, especially those in the less fertile northern part of Russia, supplemented their incomes from agriculture by engaging in handicrafts or petty trade. Others, usually with permission, worked away from their home villages in a wide variety of occupations on a seasonal or semi-permanent basis.

1 Legal status

Serfs were a particular, legally-defined category of peasants. They lived on the landed estate of members of the nobility. (The rest of the peasant population lived on land belonging to the state: state peasants – or members of the imperial family: appanage peasants.) Serfs were bound to the estates of noble landowners and were not permitted to leave without permission. Serfs were also the property of the landowners, who could buy and sell them as if they were slaves. Landowners could also take serfs away from the land and convert them to domestic serfs, who worked as servants in the landowners' households, and in a variety of skilled occupations on the estate. By 1858, domestic serfs comprised 6.8% of the serf population.

2 Land and obligation

Most landowners granted their serfs (with the exception of domestic serfs) the use of allotments of land, although legally the land remained the property of the nobles. Serfs performed obligations in return for the use of their allotments. There were two forms of these obligations. The first was labour obligations (*barshchina*). Some landowners retained part of the estate for themselves (the *demesne*), and compelled their serfs to spend part of their time cultivating this land. In 1797 Tsar Paul recommended, with limited results, that *barshchina* be restricted to three days a week.

The second category of obligations was dues (*obrok*). Some landowners turned over most of their estates to the serfs, and demanded dues in money and/or agricultural produce in return. On some estates, the two forms of obligations were combined. An unfortunate group of serfs on such estates were liable to both forms of obligations. Male serfs were also required to pay the poll tax to the state, and were liable to be conscripted into the army.

3 Landowners' authority

In addition to owning land populated by serfs, landowners were also responsible for administration and justice on their estates. In practice, however, many landowners were absentees. They hired managers or stewards to administer their estates. Most landowners used some of their serfs to help run their estates, and turned over some of the responsibilities to the serfs themselves, to the institutions known as communes (*mir* or *obshchina*). Communes took the responsibility for apportioning the allotments of land to individual serf families, and sharing out the obligations and taxes.

These four points – the serfs' legal status, their use of land allotments, their obligations to landowners, and the landowners' administrative and judicial authority – were the four main features of the institution of serfdom in Russia. This was the institution which was abolished in 1861.

Terms of abolition

The statute abolishing serfdom was signed into law by Tsar Alexander II on 19 February 1861, and published on 5 March. The eventual aim was for former serfs to become the full legal owners of allotments of land. The statute laid down a complex, gradual, three-stage process for the abolition of serfdom and transition to this new agrarian order. The first stage began on 5 March 1861. All former serfs in Russia entered a transition period, lasting from two to nine years. In this period everything, with one important exception, remained exactly as it was while preparations were made for the second stage. This was to be called 'temporary obligation', during which relations between former serfs and landowners were to be regulated by law according to charters which had been drawn up during the preceding period. 'Temporary obligation' would end when the landowner chose to initiate the third and final stage, the 'redemption operation'. During this stage former serfs would purchase land allotments from the landowners through the intermediary of the government. In 1881 the government made transfer to the final stage compulsory for all former serfs who were still 'temporarily obligated'.

The following account of the process of abolition will summarise the main terms as they related to the four main features of serfdom and to the three stages outlined above. The one thing which changed at once was the legal status of the former serfs. On 5 March 1861 serfs became legally free; they ceased to be serfs (therefore in the rest of this article they will be referred to simply as 'peasants'). Legal freedom meant, for example, that they could no longer be bought and sold, and could enter into legally binding contracts, including the sale and purchase of property, without the landowners' permission. The former domestic serfs received personal freedom, but nothing else.

During the transition period, the size and location of the peasants' land allotments remained the same as they had been immediately prior to 1861. In the second stage, 'temporary obligation', the size and location of allotments were to be set according to principles laid down in the statute, and recorded in the charters. These principles took account of local customs, regional differences and financial considerations. The statute laid down maximum and minimum sizes for peasants' allotments in each region. In some cases, however, peasants had previously cultivated allotments which were larger than the maximum size. In such cases, part of the peasants' land was taken away ('cut off') and retained by the landowners. Some historians have calculated that in the more fertile parts of Russia, where land was more valuable, peasants lost around a quarter of their land.

In the third stage, the 'redemption operation', the peasants could buy, or 'redeem', their land allotments. As most peasants lacked the resources to buy the land directly from the landowners, or even raise the money themselves in loans, the government stepped in to act as intermediary. The government agreed to advance most of the price set for the land to the landowners in long-term bonds. The peasants would then repay the money to the government, with interest capitalised at 6% per annum, in instalments. The instalments were known as redemption payments, and were to be spread over 49 years. At the end of this period, the peasants would be the full legal owners of their land allotments. In fact, the peasants quickly ran up massive arrears. The redemption payments were rescheduled, but the outstanding amount was cancelled in the aftermath of the 1905 revolution.

The peasants' obligations to the landowners remained as before during the transition period. In the second stage, 'temporary obligation', they were set by law and recorded in the charters. Obligations ceased only in the third stage, the redemption operation, when they were replaced by the redemption payments. The redemption payments were ostensibly payments for the allotments of land. In reality, however, the peasants were paying more than the market value of the land. The difference was a partly hidden element to compensate landowners for the loss of the free labour of their former serfs, or the loss of their *obrok* payments.

In the area of the fourth feature of serfdom, administration and justice, the authority of the landowners over their former serfs was handed over to a reconstituted commune at the village level, and to newly-created institutions of peasant self-government at the slightly higher level of township (*volost*). This local peasant self-government was, however, subject to the supervision of officials from the local nobility and the provincial local government institutions. Moreover, there were major reforms of local government and the courts in mid-1860s.

Peasant reaction

This summary of the terms of the abolition of serfdom cannot convey the true complexity of the reform. The statute ran to over 350 pages. The Tsar tried to explain the reform to the population in a short proclamation, which was read out in churches all over Russia during Lent. Alexander II put forward his reasons for abolishing serfdom, explained how the statute had been prepared, and summarised the terms in a rather general and unsystematic manner.[1]

1 A much misunderstood proclamation

In the weeks after the proclamation was read out, peasants all over Russia tried to make sense of what they had heard. The atmosphere in the Volga region of south-eastern Russia in the spring of 1861 was described in a letter by a landowner in Saratov province:

> Nobody could understand [the proclamation]. We have still not received the full text of the law. This has given the opportunity for everyone to interpret it in his own way. Confusion has begun. But first it was understood that freedom was postponed for two years. But as you know not all landlords are the same, but many are wicked . . . It is easily understandable that when the [proclamation] was read, peasants [belonging to the latter sort] could not believe that all the Tsar's mercy just consisted of them having to remain under this oppression for another two years . . . The peasants interpreted the [proclamation] to mean that, as they had been given freedom, there was no more labour service (completely logical, in my opinion) and stopped working for the landlords . . . The district administrator was sent to try to persuade them, but without success. The peasants respectfully told him 'Sir, we cannot disobey the Tsar's orders', and did not go to work.[2]

There were hundreds of such incidents in villages all over Russia in the spring and summer of 1861. For the most part, however, peasants restricted themselves to passive resistance. In the village of Bezdna, in Kazan province to the east of Moscow, a semi-literate peasant named Anton Petrov read the statute. He interpreted it to mean that the Tsar had granted 'true freedom', but that this was being concealed by the landowners. In part, his misinterpretation can be explained by the facts that the legislation was very complex and he was, at best, semi-literate. It is a measure of his level of literacy that he misunderstood a percentage symbol (%) to be the seal of St Anne, which he apparently believed meant that the Tsar had granted freedom. A series of officials tried without success to make the peasants see reason. Troops were sent to the village. Confronted by an enormous crowd of sullen peasants, the troops panicked and opened fire. Around 100 peasants were killed.

2 Reasons for misunderstandings

The peasants' apparent misunderstandings of the Tsar's intentions and the incidents which followed can be explained by a number of factors. The terms of abolition were extremely complex, and were not adequately explained in the proclamation which was read out.

The text is permeated by the Tsar's desire to reassure the nobility and maintain order, rather than to give a clear, concise explanation of what was going to happen to the peasants who were being freed from serfdom. Some of the priests who read out the proclamation, moreover, were probably semi-literate, and may not have read it out correctly.

The legislation was prepared and written by educated bureaucrats in St Petersburg. They drew up the legislation on the basis of lengthy discussions and debates inside the bureaucracy and with members of the nobility, and on the basis of detailed statistical research into the conditions of life on serf estates. Many of the bureaucrats, however, had little if any direct experience of peasant life. The resulting legislation was therefore written from an abstract and theoretical point of view, and was couched in difficult, legalistic terminology.

Peasants approached abolition from a very different perspective. The concerns and attitudes of the bureaucrats were completely alien to them. Most peasants had little experience of life outside the village and outside the basic features of peasant life. They knew about the customs and traditions of peasant family and village life. They understood subsistence farming and that they were compelled to serve obligations to their landowner and the Tsar. But they understood all these in purely practical terms, in the ways they affected their everyday lives. This gap between the perspectives and language of the bureaucrats who drew up the legislation and the peasants whom it affected contributed greatly to the misunderstandings and confusion which followed the promulgation of the reform. Peasants had to try to relate what they had heard read out to the experience of their daily lives.

Another reason for the misunderstandings was that serfdom was not abolished primarily in the interests of the peasantry. Rather, it was a compromise between the interests of the government, the landowning nobility and, lastly, the serfs. No one involved in preparing the reform asked serfs about their views. The authorities were interested in what serfs wanted and expected, but they were probably motivated by the desire to avert, and prepared to suppress, any serious peasant unrest which may have been caused by mass peasant disappointment with the terms of abolition. There was thus a large gulf between what was enacted in 1861 and serfs' hopes and expectations.

3 Serf expectations

One way in which peasants responded to this gulf was to try to examine the texts of proclamation and statute in more detail. Most peasants were illiterate, therefore they turned to people who were literate, and whom they thought they could trust, such as Anton Petrov, to read the legislation for them. In addition to his difficulty in reading the complex language of the statute, Anton Petrov's misunderstanding also resulted from his, and the other peasants', desire to find in the legislation what they wanted and expected.

Earlier in the nineteenth century, many serfs may have accepted any measure which seemed to promise some amelioration in their status and condition. After the public announcement of the Tsar's intention to abolish serfdom in 1857, however, they had come to hope for, and to expect, major changes. Several Soviet historians have tried to reconstruct serfs' hopes and expectations at the time of abolition. The most extreme version of serfs' demands put forward by Soviet historians was as follows:

- To become completely independent from their landowner, i.e. to become personally free.
- To be given their land allotments without payment, and also to be given all other land on the estate belonging to the landowner. It seems that serfs had their own concept of landownership. They apparently believed that they already owned the land by virtue of having cultivated it for generations.
- An end to all obligations for their landowners and to the state. They wanted to be left alone to enjoy the fruits of their own labours.
- In a similar vein, they wanted to be left alone to run their own affairs as they saw fit, in accordance with peasant customs and traditions. They did not want any supervision or interference from outside, especially not from members of the local nobility.

Less extreme variants of serfs' hopes and expectations on the eve of 1861 differ from these in degree rather than substance. The terms of the abolition of serfdom, however, were a very long way from even the less extreme variants. Only the first point, personal freedom, was granted in 1861. From the peasants' point of view the changes proposed in the other areas were a very long way from what they wanted, and were postponed far into the future. At first, immediately after the promulgation of the reform, it seems that many peasants simply could not believe that the terms of abolition were the real ones. This problem of understanding was exacerbated because many peasants believed, or at least claimed to believe, that the Tsar was on their side, and wanted to enact major reforms for their benefit.

The peasants' immediate reaction to abolition was confusion, bewilderment and disbelief. Gradually, especially after 1863, they came to accept that the terms which had been explained to them were genuine. The great hopes and expectations of 1861 died down. Peasants realised that, as they had done for centuries, they would have to continue trying to make the best of their lot, waiting for other opportunities to realise their aims and aspirations.

Notes

(1) For a translation of the proclamation, see: B. Dmytryshyn (ed.) (3rd edn) *Imperial Russia: A Source Book, 1700–1917* (Holt, Rinehart and Winston Inc, 1990), pp. 307–11.

(2) Quoted in McCauley, M. & Waldron, P. *The Emergence of the Modern Russian State, 1855–81* (Barnes and Noble Books, 1988), p. 113.

Further Reading

Blum, J. *Lord and Peasant in Russia from the Ninth to the Nineteenth Century* (Princeton University Press, 1961).

Emmons, T. 'The peasant and emancipation' in W.S. Vucinich (ed.) *The Peasant in Nineteenth-Century Russia* (Stanford University Press, 1968), pp. 41–71.

Field, D. (2nd edn) *Rebels in the Name of the Tsar* (Unwin Hyman, 1989).

Hoch, S.L. *Serfdom and Social Control in Russia: Petrovskoe, A Village in Tambov* (Chicago University Press, 1986).

Kolchin, P. *Unfree Labor: American Slavery and Russian Serfdom* (Harvard University Press, 1987).

Perrie, M. *Alexander II: Emancipation and Reform in Russia, 1855–1881* (Historical Association, 1989).

Puskarev, S.G. 'The Russian peasants' reaction to the Emancipation of 1861', *Russian Review*, Vol. 27, No. 2 (April 1968) pp. 199–214.

Zaionchkovsky, P. *The Abolition of Serfdom in Russia* (Academic International Press, 1978).

David Moon is a lecturer in the History Department at the University of Newcastle upon Tyne. He is the author of *Russian Peasants and Tsarist Legislation on the Eve of Reform: Interaction between Peasants and Officialdom, 1825–1855* (Macmillan, 1992).

PART II
Nationalism and the Breakup of the Vienna Settlement

Nations are cultural units, made up of people sharing a common language and a certain collective memory; states are political entities made up of people who live under the same government. Nationalism is the belief that all nations should be states. The inhabitants of England, though not of Ireland, take such a correspondence for granted, which is why they often find it hard to understand nationalist fervour. However, in continental Europe, states were built around common allegiance to a dynasty, a Prince or a religion. Such states did not possess the natural frontiers that were created by mountains, rivers or the sea and they did not necessarily encompass people who felt any natural sense of kinship with each other. The Habsburg Empire held together a variety of different nationalities until 1918; the Holy Roman Empire continued to exist until 1806. In nineteenth century Italy and Germany people who felt themselves to belong to the same nation were scattered among a number of smaller states. Even the idea of national language arrived comparatively late in parts of central Europe: Hungarian public business was conducted in Latin until 1848.

Nationalism is often associated with two other ideologies which became important in the nineteenth century: democracy and liberalism. In fact the connections with both were tenuous. Nationalist leaders often talked of the 'people', and occasionally they did mobilise popular support. Garibaldi earned the help of the Sicilian peasantry with a promise of land reform; the German ruling classes sought to use nationalism to undercut popular support for socialism – though there is not much evidence that they succeeded. More frequently, however, the people were violently opposed to nationalism. The Naples mob in the early nineteenth century could be relied on to attack almost any 'progressive' movement supported by their social superiors, while the Polish peasantry massacred the aristocrats who were behind the nationalist rising of 1846.

It is easy to see why nationalism and democracy came into

conflict. The 'national' culture to which idealist young men aspired was in fact the culture of an educated élite. It was a culture based on poetry and history that was learned at university. Even the language on which nations were based was often the preserve of the educated. As Jonathan Morris points out, only 3% of the Italian population spoke anything that might be recognised as Italian. Even in France, a relatively homogeneous nation, many Breton peasants would have found it easier to understand Welsh than French. In the Austrian army linguistic divisions between the educated élite and the rank and file were so great that officers sometimes gave orders in English. Some times racial and national differences between élites and people were widened by the spread of élite nationalism. The nationalist Magyar aristocracy in Hungary regarded the national minorities within their own borders with deep contempt. The nationalist German lawyers and intellectuals who met in the Frankfurt parliament of 1848 showed similar contempt for the claims of Slav nationalists. Not surprisingly, the leaders of unified Germany cared little for the Polish speakers who made up a significant part of their population and whose numbers were increased by immigration into industrial areas – the Ruhr mining basin contained 20,000 Polish speakers by the end of the nineteenth century. Nationalism was also linked to the social interests of an educated élite. Unified nations meant unified administrative structures in which the 'surplus of educated men' might hope to find jobs. Language was often important in terms of employment: Alan Sked has suggested that the 'nationalism' of the north Italian aristocracy was linked to their inability to get jobs in the German speaking civil service of their Austrian rulers.

The links between nationalism and liberalism were slightly more solid. Both took root among the property owning and educated classes. Both ideologies were hostile to the complicated overlapping jurisdictions of the old feudal orders. Both were preoccupied by taxation and the desire to abolish tariffs and this provided, for a time, a common cause for nationalists and liberals in Germany. However, there were also crucial differences between nationalists and liberals which became increasingly apparent as the nineteenth century proceeded. Liberals justified themselves in terms of rationalism and frequently espoused a cultural view that was rooted in the classicism of the eighteenth century. Nationalism was connected to the irrational culture of romanticism; it is hard to imagine that the need for balanced budgets would have filled Byron with the same ardour as the campaign for Greek independence. The split between nationalism and liberalism was exposed by the Napoleonic Wars. Liberals often supported the French forces, which they associated with 'liberty' and the spread of orderly centralised administration. Nationalists, on the other hand, resented the extension of the Napoleonic Empire.

The link between liberalism and nationalism raises the question of the economic basis of national unifications. Economic advances often facilitated such unifications. In particular, railways made unification seem more urgent by integrating areas, as well as providing another potential national bureaucracy and source of employment. German unification was particularly tied up with economic growth and with Prussia's need to gain access to the raw materials found in other parts of Germany. Keynes remarked that Germany was unified 'more by coal and iron than by blood and iron.' However, Germany was unified around 'national economics' that stressed the need for protection from other countries through tariffs; the key figure in German unification, Bismarck, turned his back on the liberals who had been his early allies. Italy, by contrast, saw a continuation of the alliance between liberalism and nationalism throughout the unification period, and the Italian liberalism did not begin to lose power until the late nineteenth century. Italian liberals expected the underdeveloped Italian economy to grow and prosper without state intervention: they were disappointed. After political unification, the Italian economy remained fragmented – indeed, in some respects, the gap between industrialised northern cities like Turin and the South grew. Disillusion with the economic consequences of liberalism in Italy, and elsewhere, partly explains why nationalism ultimately came to take the more radical form of fascism.

Richard Clogg
The Greek War of Independence

The end of the Cold War saw the re-emergence of Nationalism in the Balkans. Richard Clogg illustrates that Nationalism has a long history in this part of Europe.

As during the decades that preceded the outbreak of the First World War, the Balkan peninsula again became convulsed by nationalism after the end of the Cold War. The Balkans provide a striking example of the destructive consequences of nationalism in a region where national and ethnic boundaries have seldom corresponded. For this reason it is instructive to look at the movement for Greek independence during the late eighteenth and early nineteenth centuries. For it was the Greeks who introduced the phenomenon of nationalism to the Balkans.

It is true that the Serb revolt of 1804, which resulted in the gaining of a certain autonomy *vis-à-vis* the Ottoman Empire in 1815, anteceded the Greek war of independence, but the Serbs in the initial stages of their uprising lacked the consciously nationalist motives that inspired some, if by no means all, of those Greeks who raised the standard of revolt against the Ottoman Turks in Moldavia, the northernmost of the two Danubian Principalities, and in the Peloponnese in the early months of 1821. What were the reasons for the relative precocity of the Greek national movement and what were its salient features? Geography is one factor. Although internal communications in the mountainous regions inhabited by Greeks were as poor as they were elsewhere in the Balkan peninsula, nonetheless the enormous coastline of the Greek lands and the numerous Aegean islands, with their very largely Greek populations, meant that the Greeks were more open to trading and other influences from Western Europe than were the more land-locked peoples of the peninsula. A strong nautical tradition, which continues to this day, developed in certain of the islands and the prosperous mercantile marine that emerged in the decades before 1821 gave the Greeks an important advantage when the armed struggle broke out. Greeks gained control of the sea early in the conflict, and fire ships were used to great effect against the cumbersome ships-of-the-line of the Ottoman fleet.

Greeks under Ottoman rule

At the same time the very structure of the Ottoman state privileged the Greek inhabitants of this vast multi-ethnic empire. The Ottomans exercised control over their numerous subject populations who were not Muslim by belief through the *millet* system. The various millets were constituted on the basis of religion rather than ethnic origin. Thus, in addition to the ruling Muslim millet, there was a Jewish millet, a Gregorian Armenian millet and, much the largest, the *millet-i Rum*, or 'Greek' millet, as the Turks called it. This was a misnomer, for it embraced all the Sultan's subjects of the Orthodox faith. That is to say, besides Greeks, it included Bulgarians, Serbs, Romanians and their Vlach kin, and those not insignificant numbers of Albanians and Arabs who were Orthodox Christians. Nonetheless the title, even if inaccurate, did reflect an important reality, namely that the millet-i Rum was dominated by the Greeks. The Ecumenical Patriarch (who was based in the Ottoman capital, Istanbul or Constantinople) and the upper reaches of the Orthodox hierarchy, through which the millet was governed, were invariably Greek. This degree of Greek control of the Orthodox millet increasingly came to be resented by its non-Greek members and, in the nineteenth century, was to prove a powerful stimulus to the national movements of the other Balkan peoples who wanted to establish national churches of their own.

The Patriarch and his senior clerics were granted a wide degree of authority over the affairs of the millet which enjoyed a considerable degree of freedom in religious matters. In return the Patriarch, as head of the millet, was expected to act as the guarantor of the loyalty of his flock to the Sultan. When the armed struggle for independence broke out in 1821, the then Patriarch Grigorios V, out of conviction not mere expediency, condemned the insurgents in the strongest terms. But he was nonetheless hung in reprisal at one of the gates of the Patriarchate, a gate that has never since been opened. This was seen in Western Europe as a characteristic instance of Ottoman barbarism but, in Ottoman eyes, Grigorios had failed in his primary duty, that of ensuring the loyalty of his flock towards the Sultan.

Greeks, besides their control over the affairs of the Orthodox millet, occupied other positions of privilege and influence within the empire. Between the beginning of the eighteenth century and 1821, Phanariot Greeks, forming a kind of *noblesse de robe* and drawn from a small group of Greek or Hellenised families from the Ottoman capital, monopolised a number of important offices in the Ottoman state structure. Phanariot *hospodars* or princes ruled as the viceroys of the Ottomans over the Danubian principalities of

Wallachia and Moldavia. They acquired a reputation as oppressors of the native Romanians, but they also acted as patrons of learning and their sumptuous courts to an extent acted as channels of western influence. Phanariot Greek grandees controlled two other high offices of state, that of principal interpreter to the Ottoman Porte (government) and that of principal interpreter to the Grand Admiral of the Ottoman fleet. Both offices were more influential than they sound. The principal interpreter to the Porte acted as a kind of deputy foreign minister, while the interpreter to the fleet also acted effectively as governor of the Aegean isles, from whose Greek inhabitants many of the sailors in the Ottoman fleet were drawn.

Thus, in the decades before 1821, Greeks enjoyed a privileged position in the Ottoman power structure *vis-à-vis* the other Balkan Christians. But the Phanariots tended to identify with the interests of their Ottoman masters. More important to the development of the national movement was the emergence in the eighteenth century of a Greek mercantile middle class, which came to control much of the commerce of the empire. Most of the wealthier merchants were, like the Phanariots, too firmly wedded to the existing status quo to offer much direct support to the embyronic national movement. But, by endowing schools and libraries, by subsidising a growing (and increasingly secular) literature published for a Greek readership, and by sponsoring the studies of promising young students in the universities of Western Europe (and particularly of Germany), they effectively underwrote the intellectual revival that was such a characteristic feature of the 50 years or so before 1821.

Rediscovering the past

A distinctive feature of this revival was a rediscovery of the heritage of ancient Greece. During the dark years of the *Tourkokratia*, or period of Turkish rule, there had been little awareness of the classical past. Those who studied abroad, however, in addition to coming into contact with the intoxicating ideas of the Enlightenment and of the French Revolution, soon became aware of the extent to which the civilisation of ancient Greece was revered throughout Western Europe and, indeed, in the United States, where ancient Greek came near to being adopted as the official language. By contrast, virtually nothing was known of the historical antecedents of the other Balkan peoples.

This renewed sense of the past manifested itself in a number of ways; in the publishing of classical Greek texts for a modern Greek readership (an undertaking in which Adamantios Korais, a Greek from Smyrna who lived much of his life in Paris, played a leading role) and in the adoption of classical Greek first names (e.g. Pericles and Aspasia), nowadays a common practice but one that was unknown before the early 1800s. This enthusiasm for the ancient world aroused the wrath of the Orthodox Church, which equated ancient culture (and the learning of the European Enlightenment) with paganism. Conversely the way in which the the Orthodox hierarchy preached the need for absolute obedience to the Ottoman state, which it saw as a bulwark helping to protect Orthodoxy from being undermined by the pernicious heresies of the West, angered the nascent nationalist intelligentsia.

This intelligentsia remained small, and much of it was based in the diaspora communities that had grown up outside the Greek lands. Most of those living within the Greek lands saw themselves as Orthodox Christians rather than as Greeks; the process of forging a specifically Greek national identity among the mass of the population came after, rather than before, independence. Aspirations for an eventual liberation from the Turkish yoke were kept alive at a popular level by prophecies and messianic beliefs that held out the hope of emancipation through divine rather than human agency.

The depredations of the *klefts* (literally 'thieves') constituted a kind of primitive resistance to Ottoman rule. Essentially outlaws who attacked Greek and Turk alike, the klefts, because their targets were often such visible symbols of Ottoman rule as tax collectors, came in the popular mind to be seen as the defenders of the oppressed Greeks against their Muslim rulers. Moreover, by the late eighteenth century large areas of the Ottoman Empire had passed from the control of the central government to provincial notables known as *ayans*. Perhaps the best known of these was Ali Pasha, who from his power base in Jannina ruled over large areas of what is now Albania and mainland Greece. Ali's successful and prolonged defiance of the Porte afforded a suggestive example to those plotting the liberation of their homeland.

Planning for insurgency

Many of the élites of pre-independence Greek society were too comfortably locked into the existing system to want to challenge Ottoman authority. By the end of the eighteenth century, however, some bold spirits were beginning to contemplate an armed struggle, however overwhelming the odds. One such was Rigas Velestinlis, who during a sojourn in Vienna had been powerfully influenced by the French Revolution. He devised a plan for what was, in effect, a revived Byzantine Empire, but with republican institutions on the French model substituted for monarchical. In 1797 he set out to preach the gospel of revolution throughout the Balkans. But before

73

he had even left Habsburg territory he was arrested in Trieste and handed over, together with those of his fellow conspirators who were Ottoman subjects, to the Turks, who had him strangled in the fortress of Belgrade in May 1798. If nothing came of Rigas' visionary schemes he did instil a disproportionate apprehension in the Ottoman authorities, whose fears of revolutionary influence had already been aroused by the French liberation of the Ionian Islands in 1797 and were to be further heightened by Bonaparte's occupation of Egypt in 1798.

If Rigas' schemes had no practical outcome his martyrdom was to inspire succeeding generations of nationalists. His example was certainly in the minds of the founders of the *Philiki Etairia*, the Friendly Society, established in 1814 by three young Greeks in Odessa, an important centre of Greek commerce in Southern Russia. The aim of the conspirators was the liberation of the homeland, which was to be accomplished by armed revolt. The Society, whose elaborate initiation rituals were strongly influenced by Freemasonry, made little headway in the early years.

In seeking recruits the conspirators played on the widespread popular belief among the Greeks that the *xanthon genos*, a fair-haired race of northerners universally identified with the Russians, the only sovereign Orthodox power, would one day emerge as their liberators. But the Russians were not party to the plot, whose leadership was twice declined by Ioannis Capodistrias, the Corfiote Greek who served as the joint foreign minister of Tsar Alexander I. Capodistrias counselled the Greeks to await one of the frequent wars between the Russian and Ottoman Empires when the Greeks might hope to emerge with the kind of autonomous status that had been secured by the Serbs. The supreme leadership of the Philiki Etairia passed instead to General Alexander Ypsilantis, a Phanariot Greek in the service of the Tsar. Grandiose schemes were elaborated which would have involved Serbs and Bulgars in the planned uprising, but the other Balkan peoples showed little enthusiasm for the substitution of Greek for Turkish hegemony.

The outbreak of the revolt

It was the attempt by Sultan Mahmud II to crush Ali Pasha during the winter of 1820–21 that was to give the Philiki Etairia the chance to launch a revolt, for substantial Ottoman forces were tied up in the campaign. Alexander Ypsilantis, characteristically invoking the glories of ancient Greece, therefore launched an invasion of Moldavia across the Pruth river from Russian territory in early March 1821, while an almost simultaneous uprising also occurred in the Peloponnese. The Moldavian insurgency was soon crushed at the

Battle of Dragatsani in June, and Ypsilantis was forced to flee into exile and captivity in the Habsburg Empire.

The Peloponnesian uprising, however, at the outset met with a considerable degree of success. The element of surprise, the long tradition of kleftic warfare and control of the sea all worked to the Greeks' advantage. With both sides giving no quarter, the Turks were forced to withdraw to their coastal fortresses. Despite these initial successes the struggle was to prove a protracted one. The governments of the Europe of the Holy Alliance showed scant sympathy for what they perceived as a threat to the established order. By contrast, liberal opinion in Europe embraced the Greek cause with enthusiasm. Soon philhellene volunteers, the poet Byron among them, began to make their way to Greece. They numbered in their ranks genuine idealists, assorted cranks and do-gooders and some out and out rogues. A few became disillusioned when the modern Greeks failed to match up to their romanticised and idealised image of their ancient forebears. Philhellenic committees in Europe and North America raised funds for the insurgents. If the military contribution of the philhellenes to the conflict was mixed, their activities did boost Greek morale and, in some small way, contribute to a climate in which the Great Powers eventually felt obliged to intervene in the conflict.

Strife among the insurgents

Partly with a view to impressing enlightened opinion in Europe the insurgents early in 1822 adopted a constitution that, on paper, was highly democratic for its time. In 1823 this was revised and the three local governments that had come into existence in the liberated territories were fused into one centralised authority. But factionalism among the insurgents was to threaten the conduct of the struggle and, in 1824, was to lead to outright civil war. The underlying reasons for this internecine strife are complex, with political alignments and alliances shifting over time. The Peloponnesian notables, 'Christian Turks' as their opponents derisively termed them, were anxious to retain the substantial power and privileges that they had enjoyed under the Turks. This brought them into conflict with the kleftic leaders, Theodoros Kolokotronis prominent among them, who felt that their military contribution to the war deserved greater recognition and a corresponding share of political power. Similar demands were made by the island ship owners whose contribution to the war at sea was considerable. The small nationalist intelligentsia lacked political muscle, but sought to endow the emerging state with the trappings of liberal constitutionalism.

The power struggles among the insurgents can be seen as reflecting antagonisms between a 'civilian' or 'aristocratic' party (the Peloponnesian notables, the ship owners, and the small group of Phanariots who had thrown their lot in with the insurgents) on the one hand and a 'military' or 'democratic' party (with the kleftic leaders representing the popular interest) on the other.

The feuding can also be interpreted in terms of a clash between traditional élites and modernisers. The traditionalists, who looked on the struggle essentially as a religious crusade against the Muslim Turks, were not fighting for political democracy. Rather they sought to substitute their own oligarchical rule for that of the Turks. The modernisers, conscious nationalists, wanted to introduce liberal constitutionalism to Greece, to develop a European-type army and to curb the traditional prerogatives of the church. These radically different world-views were reflected in lifestyle, and indeed in dress, as well as ideology. The westernisers would dress in European clothes, the old élites stuck to their richly embroidered waistcoats and the traditional *foustanella*, a kind of kilt.

The intervention of the powers

Schisms of this kind boded ill for the prosecution of the war. The military fortunes of the insurgents deteriorated rapidly when Sultan Mahmud II enlisted the support of his nominal vassal Mehmet Ali, the ruler of Egypt, and of his son Ibrahim Pasha, in return for the promise of rich territorial compensation, including the island of Crete. What saved the Greek cause was the reluctant involvement of the Great Powers. Their commercial interests in the region had been severely damaged by the continuing hostilities, while each was fearful lest the other should exploit the crisis to its own advantage.

Britain and Russia agreed on joint mediation in the Protocol of St Petersburg of 1826, and France became a party through the Treaty of London of 1827. Thus was inaugurated the ambiguous policy categorised by George Canning as one of peaceful interference. This culminated in the destruction of the Turkish-Egyptian fleet by a combined British, Russian and French fleet at the Battle of Navarino in October 1827, the last great battle of the age of sail. Although some form of independence for Greece was now inevitable it was to be some years, however, before the frontiers of the new state were to be agreed and before the Protecting Powers, Britain, France and Russia, were to guarantee the existence of an independent Greek state.

The fact that the new state which formally came into existence in 1832 contained within its borders barely a third of the Greek inhabitants of the Ottoman Empire was to mean that its foreign relations, and indeed domestic politics, were to be dominated for much of the first century of its existence by the *Megali Idea*, the Great Idea of incorporating within the bounds of a single state, whose capital would be Constantinople, all the Greek populations of the Near East. This irredentist project was necessarily to bring Greece into conflict with the Ottoman Empire. Moreover as the other Balkan peoples followed the Greek example and themselves sought independence, there was inevitable antagonism between these emergent states as they sought to acquire as large a share as possible of the Balkan possessions of the Ottoman Empire. It was the Greeks who introduced the spark of nationalism to the Balkans. The explosive consesquences are with us to the present day.

Further Reading

Clogg, R. (ed. and trans.) *The Movement for Greek Independence 1770–1821: A Collection of Documents* (Macmillan, 1976).

Clogg, R. *A Concise History of Greece* (Cambridge University Press, 1992).

Crawley, C.W. *The Question of Greek Independence: A Study of British Policy in the Near East, 1821–33* (Cambridge University Press, 1930).

Dakin, D. *The Greek Struggle for Independence, 1821–33* (Batsford, 1973).

Henderson, G.P. *The Revival of Greek Thought 1620–1830* (Scottish Academic Press, 1971).

Lidderdale, H.A. (trans.) *The Memoirs of General Makriyannis 1797–1864* (Oxford University Press, 1966).

Woodhouse, C.M. *The Battle of Navarino* (Hodder and Stoughton, 1973).

Woodhouse, C.M. *Capodistria: The Founder of Greek Independence, 1821–9* (Oxford University Press, 1973).

Zkythinos, D.A. *The Making of Modern Greece: From Byzantium to Independence* (Blackwell, 1976).

Richard Clogg is an Associate Fellow of St Antony's College, Oxford and Professor of Modern Balkan History at the University of London. He is the author of *A Concise History of Greece* (Cambridge University Press, 1992).

Jonathan Morris
The Risorgimento's Failure: Italian Unification and After

Italian unification has traditionally featured on A-level syllabuses as a 'liberal success' of mid-nineteenth century Europe. But how successful was it, and how united was the new Italy that emerged?

Whilst the drama of the unification of Italy, the so-called *risorgimento*, makes a regular appearance in A-level courses, what followed is rarely explored. This is a shame, because the 'after' enables us to understand much more about the nature of the *risorgimento* itself. Why has the period been so under-explored? Perhaps it is because, as Benedetto Croce suggested, the poetry of unification was followed by the prose of actually constructing a nation-state. D'Azeglio's famous epigram: 'We have made Italy, now we must make Italians', pointed to the new challenge for the governments of united Italy, yet the mass of Italians remained as unconnected to, and as resentful of, their new rulers, as they had been of the various regimes they had previously experienced. Given the failure of Italy's rulers to integrate the people into the political system, some historians now deny that there was a *risorgimento*, that is to say a moment of national rebirth, at all.

Cavour, Liberalism and the Constitution

So how should we understand what happened during Italian unification? The *risorgimento* is sometimes held to have begun with the uprisings of 1848. On 18 March, the people of Milan took to the streets and after five days of fighting, forced the Austrian garrison under Radetzky to abandon the city. Encouraged by Cavour and his colleagues at the newspaper *Il Risorgimento*, Charles Albert, the King of Piedmont, entered Lombardy in order to engage the Austrians. Subsequently popular uprisings broke out throughout Italy, notably in Venice, Naples and Rome.

Yet one could argue that the real beginning of the *risorgimento* was 4 March 1848, when Charles Albert issued a constitution, *lo statuto*, again as a result of pressure from Cavour. The main feature of the constitution was the establishment of a parliament with effective control over the budget, but the parliament itself was elected on a very narrow franchise largely based on wealth and position.

Liberals argued that by vesting the right to vote in the possession of a large amount of property or a state office which required a considerable degree of learning, the constitution ensured that only men who were not subject to undue influence – such as that which could have been exercised by employers, for instance – were able to vote. In practice, of course, it meant that government reflected the overall interests of the élite classes by which it was elected.

From Cavour's point of view, part of the attraction of lo statuto was that it incorporated into the political system a bourgeois élite which might otherwise have turned to the masses for support. Many of the original leaders of the 1848 protests were alarmed by the extent of the demands for social change that the uprisings unleashed. Members of the bourgeoisie in Venice, for instance, undoubtedly viewed the restoration of Austrian dominance with some relief. One could argue, therefore, that the introduction of the Piedmontese constitution was a form of conservative revolution, transforming the nature of government in order to avoid the entry of the masses into politics.

The importance of lo statuto became clear in the years after 1849. The liberal bourgeoisie of Piedmont were both instigators and beneficiaries of the economic upturn of the mid-nineteenth century which, in turn, supported an efficient bureaucracy of officials who were loyal to a state in which they had a stake as electors. Piedmont, then, provided a model of how a liberal constitutional state could function to the benefit of crown, élite and bourgeoisie, without recourse to mass politics.

This helps explain why the ruling élite in the Central Duchies and Tuscany were prepared to countenance their incorporation into the emerging Northern Italian state in 1860. Men such as Ricasoli in Tuscany and Minghetti in Emilia had been conservatives in 1849, afraid of the social demands that the protest movements had unleashed. Ten years later, however, they rallied to the risorgimento because Piedmontese leadership in effect guaranteed their interests. Although popular plebiscites sanctioned the adhesion of the Duchies to Piedmont, it is worth remembering that the negotiations over what form unification would take were carried out exclusively by representatives of the conservative landowning classes, who were more concerned with preserving their own position than building a new nation. Piedmont's successful constitutional experiment offered them a way forward.

Garibaldi, Unification and Democracy

Cavour's fear that a real risorgimento would lead to a challenge to the social order led him to try to prevent radical democrats such as

Key

- Kingdom of Sardinia in 1815
- Territory annexed, 1859
- Territory annexed, May 1860
- Territory annexed, November 1860
- Territory annexed, 1866

SAVOY

PIEDMONT (KINGDOM OF SARDINIA)

LOMBARDY

VENETIA

NICE

GENOA

PARMA

MODENA

MONACO

Territory lost to France, 1860

CORSICA French from 1768, formerly Genoese

TUSCANY

SAN MARINO

PAPAL STATES

Annexed, 1870

Adriatic Sea

KINGDOM OF SARDINIA

KINGDOM

OF THE

TWO

Mediterranean Sea

SICILIES

0   100   200 km

The Unification of Italy, 1859–70

Garibaldi and Mazzini playing much of a role in the campaign for unification. Indeed one reason that Cavour was so keen on the alliance with France in 1859 was that it removed the need to appeal for volunteers for the battle against Austria. Such an appeal would almost certainly have had to be based on the promise of the greater democracy and social reform that Cavour was anxious to avoid.

It was to carry out just such a transformation that Garibaldi organised the expedition of the 'Thousand' to Sicily. It is often argued that this was the moment in which Garibaldi, enraged by Cavour ceding Nice and Savoy to France in return for services rendered (Nice, after all, was Garibaldi's own birthplace and, to any convinced nationalist, Italian soil), outmanoeuvred the Piedmontese Prime Minister by extending the scope of the campaigns for independence to the South. In fact, the picture is somewhat more complicated. Cavour's diplomatic position, particularly his reliance on France, prevented him from endorsing the expedition, but it is clear that he let it proceed, and even allowed fund-raising activities to take place in Piedmont after its departure. Was this because he simply didn't dare to oppose what appeared to be a popular undertaking, or did he always expect to profit from the project, providing he was not associated with it? Historians are divided on the answer to this question, but it is clear that Garibaldi's expedition bequeathed to both Cavour and his successors a host of difficulties that greatly influenced the character of post-unification Italy. Three main problems can be identified.

Firstly, Garibaldi forced the inclusion into Italy of the Kingdom of the Two Sicilies, a backward region roughly equal in size to that of the rest of the territories united under Victor Emanuel in 1860. Whilst Cavour may have intended to absorb the South at some stage in his career, it seems certain that he had not intended to do so so quickly.

Secondly, the populist slogans that Garibaldi had employed during his campaign generated precisely the demands for social reform that Cavour was anxious to avoid. Garibaldi's promise of land redistribution roused peasantry whose resentment of the Bourbons had been sustained by the fact that the restoration of the dynasty had quashed similar schemes put forward under Napoleon. Instead of waiting for redistribution, the peasants began occupying the land of their own accord, much to the resentment of the landowners. As a result the southern notables, who had no particular love of the Bourbons, were extremely hostile to the new state.

Finally, by forcing Piedmont to occupy the Papal States in order to prevent him marching on Rome itself, Garibaldi provoked a rift between the Vatican and the Kingdom of Italy that led to the Pope refusing to recognise the new kingdom – a position that was

Main Events during Italian Unification

March 1848	Piedmont adopts a constitution; Charles Albert enters war with Austrians
March 1849	Austrians defeat Piedmontese at Novara
April 1859	War declared between Austria and Piedmont (joined in May by France)
July 1859	Armistice of Villafranca; Lombardy ceded to Piedmont, Venetia remains Austrian
March 1860	Plebiscites in Modena, Tuscany and Romagna favour union with Piedmont; Cavour cedes Nice and Savoy to France
May 1860	Garibaldi and 'the Thousand' land in Sicily
September 1860	Piedmontese occupy Southern Papal States
October 1860	Garibaldi presents Kingdom of Two Sicilies to Victor Emanuel II
June 1866	Italians invade Venetia after outbreak of Austro-Prussian war
September 1870	Italian troops enter Rome following withdrawal of French garrison to fight in Franco-Prussian war

maintained until Mussolini negotiated the Lateran Pacts of 1929. Catholicism was one of the few things that most Italians had in common, but the effect of this rift was to make it impossible to unite the country around religion, or to utilise this belief as the basis for a mass political party. This had profound consequences for the structure of post-unification politics.

Political structures after 1861

In October 1860, Garibaldi's forces met up with those of Victor Emanuel, leaving him little option but to deliver formally his newly-acquired territories to his sovereign. In March 1861 Victor Emanuel was formally proclaimed King of Italy: 'by the grace of God and the will of the people'. Whatever the role of the deity, however, the people had no say in the matter, and would continue not to do so.

In reality the new kingdom was little more than a remodelling of the Piedmont, as the king's insistence that he continue to be known as Victor Emanuel the Second, not the First, indicated. The new democratic Italy that Garibaldi craved was not forthcoming. The Piedmontese constitution was simply adopted as that for Italy with the result that even in 1880 the electorate comprised a mere 8% of the adult male population. Cavour's recipe for a conservative revolution was to be applied throughout Italy, with only the landowning élite, higher state officials and the small commercial and industrial bourgeoisie gaining the vote.

Yet even the notables were known to be suspicious of the new state. The variety of economic conditions pertaining throughout the peninsula meant that they often had very different outlooks to their Piedmontese counterparts, and sometimes found it difficult to distinguish between unification and colonisation by Piedmont. Aware of these problems, the government appointed officials called 'prefects' to act as its local representatives in each of the country's provinces. The prefects exercised considerable powers over local government, choosing the mayor and advising local councils how to reach decisions that were acceptable to the government. Prefects could even recommend the dismissal of the council and its replacement by a royal commissioner selected by the state.

All these controls indicated a lack of trust between the regime and élite groups throughout the new country. Significantly no layers of regional government were introduced, thereby avoiding any challenges to the national administration. Yet, because councils were also elected on a very restricted franchise, local power was left in the notables' hands so they had little need to challenge the central authorities. Indeed, recent historical writing has highlighted how far local councils were allowed to get on with pursuing their own interests providing they maintained outward co-operation with the state.

The prefects' main task was ensuring that a pro-government deputy was returned to parliament. To this end they were expected to use their powers of patronage: making sure, for example, that state contracts and appointments were given to those who turned out to vote for government candidates. If this seems corrupt and undemocratic one should remember that elections in Italy were plagued by low turnouts, indicative of the lack of acceptance of the regime, particularly amongst Catholics, who heeded the Pope's command to abstain from voting. Thus the prefects' real work was not so much getting government candidates elected, as getting the very idea of the Italian state accepted.

There were no real organised political parties, largely because, with so many deputies drawn from the same social strata, there were few clear ideological conflicts (this was particularly true after the first essentially Piedmontese administrations gave way to broader-based governments in the 1870s). A deputy's main activity was to feed back money to his constituency, thus satisfying his constituents, and insuring his own position. Politics were based on interest groups, with the leading politicians being those who were best able to build broad coalitions by absorbing potential opponents into their faction through the promise of political favours: a manoeuvre that was known as *trasformismo*. Inevitably many coalitions were short-lived as a result of the constant horse-trading that went on (there were 28 administrations between 1860 and 1892), but the best practitioners of *trasformismo* survived from one administration to the next. Agostino Depretis, for example, dominated Italian politics through his mastery of *trasformismo* between 1876 and 1887, as did Francesco Crispi between 1887 and 1896, and Giovanni Giolitti between 1901 and 1914.

A united Italy?

Italy's theoretical unity had little to do with the country's real condition. In 1861 nearly all Italians actually spoke a form of dialect as their first language, and less than 3% could speak Italian at all. When Italian school textbooks recount the words allegedly spoken by the king on his entry into Rome – 'Here we are and here we will stay' – they usually omit to mention that he was talking in Piedmontese French. Economically, the North was already much more advanced than the South, both in terms of the kinds of farming and manufacturing taking place, and the prosperity that they created. Although most Italians did share a common religion, Catholicism could not play a part in 'making Italians', given the Pope's hostility to the new state.

There were, then, a formidable number of barriers to a complete unification of Italy, but was there the will to overcome these? As we have seen, one characteristic of Cavour's blueprint for unification was not to popularise the struggle for independence so as to avoid demands for mass participation in politics and social reform. The adoption of the Piedmontese constitution created the largest of all the divisions within Italy, that between 'legal' Italy – that small portion of the population who had the vote and participated in political affairs – and the 'real Italy' of the disenfranchised masses.

'Real Italy' largely experienced unification in the form of 'Piedmontization'. The breaking down of internal trade barriers and the introduction of Piedmontese weights and measures and external tariffs was often disastrous for the economies of other regions of Italy which were unable to adjust to the new conditions. Worse still for the ordinary people was the government's insistence on the need to redress the huge budget deficits that had financed the unification armies. The *macinato*, a tax on grinding grain, was often the only contact between peasants and the new state, and it generated much unrest that frequently ended in violence.

Nowhere was this more the case than the South, where Garibaldi's promise of land redistribution generated precisely the kinds of demands that Cavour had wished to avoid. The army was repeatedly used to restore order by taking on the peasant 'outlaws' in order to return land to its original owners, and establish the authority of the new state. Although the government claimed it was fighting against 'brigandage', the truth was that it was engaged in a virtual civil war with fellow Italians. The campaigns against brigandage resulted in more lives being lost than in all the battles for unification itself – a revealing comment on the relative proportions of popular involvement and popular resistance to the *risorgimento*.

The army, however, did play one other important role in 'making Italians'. It taught all its recruits Italian, not only as a language of command, but also in its written form.

Only literate men were able to gain an early discharge. In 1882, the franchise was reformed so that literacy, rather than wealth, became the key factor in entitlement to vote. Literacy was taken to be denoted by a certain number of years attendance at school: Italy's new class of voters were essentially those who had been taught the country's language. This was clearly a project for making Italians, one which also developed the Liberal idea that only those individuals who could be relied on to exercise their vote in a rational, i.e. educated, manner should possess the franchise.

The newly-qualified voters were mainly middle-class men. Only in the more economically and educationally advanced towns of the North did a significant number of workers gain the vote. Countryside areas, particularly those in the South, were far less affected and continued to return liberal deputies who were more concerned with their constituency's interests than with national politics. The extension of the local government franchise in 1889 along similar lines reinforced this division between town and countryside. The political élite maintained its hold on the countryside, and thus on national power in the parliament, whilst accommodating demands for more progressive politics in the cities: a pattern that persisted until a further suffrage reform in 1912.

Conclusion

In effect, then, the politicians of 'legal Italy' tried to make themselves acceptable to the inhabitants of 'real Italy', but avoided integrating the latter into the political system. Mostly this was done by conciliation – notably by opening up participation in politics at the local level – but ministers did not shirk from using oppression when the occasion demanded. Crispi, for example, granted councils the right to elect their own mayors in 1896, and was initially friendly to the development of labour organisations amongst both industrial workers and peasants. Yet when their protests became violent, as in Sicily in 1894, he imposed military rule to put them down, as did his successors in 1898 when the army killed 80 workers during demonstrations in Milan.

The persistence of the division between 'legal' Italy and 'real' Italy points to the real failure of the *risorgimento*. Italy was united, Italians were not. The point is, however, that this was a deliberate failure – Cavour did not want to politicise the nation, so much as to establish a much more powerful version of the Piedmontese state, as his and his successors' attachment to the Piedmontese constitution testified. That it was this project, and not those of Garibaldi or Mazzini, that was enacted after unification perhaps explains why the period was one of prose rather than poetry, and why Italy was tempted into a very different project for national reawakening in the 1920s.

Further Reading

Clark, M. *Modern Italy 1871–1982* (Longman, 1984).

Coppa, F.J. *The Origins of the Italian Wars of Independence* (Longman, 1992).

Davis, J.A. *Conflict and Control: Law and Order in Nineteenth-Century Italy* (Macmillan, 1988).

Lovett, C. *The Democratic Movement in Italy, 1830–76* (Harvard University Press, 1982).

Riall, L. 'Elite resistance to state formation: the case of Italy' in M. Fulbrook (ed.) *National Histories and European History* (UCL Press, 1993).

Smith, D.M. (2nd edn) *The Making of Italy 1796–1870* (Macmillan, 1988).

Jonathan Morris is Lecturer in Modern European History at University College, University of London, and author of *The Political Economy of Shopkeeping in Milan 1886–1922* (Cambridge University Press, 1993).

Michael John
The Unification of Germany

The familiar textbook interpretation of German unification in the mid-nineteenth century emphasises Bismarck's role. Going beyond the textbooks, Michael John places the process of unification in its social and political context.

Historical writing on the unification of Germany in the 1860s and 1870s has tended, for fairly obvious reasons, to focus on the central role of Bismarckian power politics and the force of Prussian arms. The drama of the events of the 1860s, the revolutionary impact of Bismarck on the European state system and the seeming impotence of his opponents both at home and abroad make this type of approach understandable and, to a certain extent at least, justifiable. In perhaps the best recent biography of Bismarck, Lothar Gall has pointed to the importance of the Chancellor's early realisation in 1862 that the nationalist hopes of his liberal opponents at home might be 'instrumentalised' – i.e. that one way out of the predicament in which the Prussian monarchy found itself would be to adopt the foreign policy aspirations of the liberals (national unification on a 'small German' basis), while standing firm against the liberals' demands for political reform at home. Such an approach involved a radical revision of conventional thought concerning the relationship between domestic and foreign policy and aroused the deep suspicions of conservative forces in Prussia and elsewhere. Even those historians such as Helmut Böhme and Hans-Ulrich Wehler, who look for the roots of Bismarck's success in dynamic changes in the social and economic sphere after 1850, nevertheless implicitly confirm that Bismarck set the diplomatic timetable, so to speak, and that he made the running in a way which had fundamentally negative consequences for the development of a fully liberal political system in post-1871 Germany. By contrast, the social history of liberal nationalism and the idea that national unification constituted a social process as well as a political one has been relatively neglected by scholars and general writers on the 'German question'. As that question is now being raised in an increasingly acute form by what undoubtedly amounts to a profound social process, it may well be time to consider the other side of German national unification in the 1860s as well.

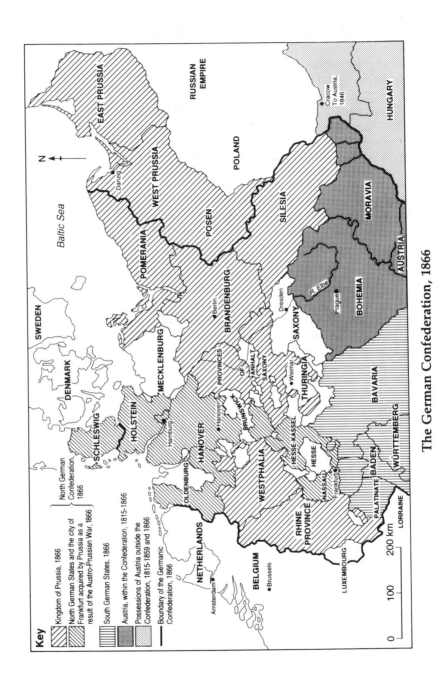

The German Confederation, 1866

Key

Kingdom of Prussia, 1866

North German States and the city of
Frankfurt acquired by Prussia as a
result of the Austro-Prussian War, 1866

North German
Confederation,
1866

South German States, 1866

Austria, within the Confederation, 1815-1866

Possessions of Austria outside the
Confederation, 1815-1859 and 1866

Boundary of the Germanic
Confederation, 1866

0   100   200 km

Main Events during German Unification

1850

April   Prussia puts forward a plan for the unification of Germany at Erfurt. Vehement opposition from Austria

May   Austrian Prime Minister, Schwarzenberg, recalls the *diet* of Frankfurt and asks the German states to reconsider revising the old German Confederation. Prussia is absent.

Nov   Convention of Olmütz. Prussia agrees to discard the Erfurt Union and accepts Austria as the supreme force in the German Confederation. Prussia humiliated.

1853

April   German Customs Union extended until 1865, but Austria is excluded.

1861

Jan   William I becomes the King of Prussia.

Feb   Progressive Party established in Prussia. Aim: to unify Germany under Prussia.

1862

Sept   Otto von Bismark becomes the minister president of Prussia. Makes 'Blood and Iron' speech on German Unification.

Dec   Bismarck informs Austria that it must accept Prussia as an equal within Germany.

1863

Sept   German princes meet at Frankfurt with the intention of reforming the German Confederation. Prussia refuses to co-operate and the meeting is disbanded.

Oct   The German *diet* agrees to act against Denmark following its annexation of Schleswig-Holstein.

Dec   Hanoverian and Saxon forces cross into Holstein.

1864

Oct   Denmark cedes Schleswig-Holstein to Austrian and Prussia who are to decide what to do with the two Duchies.

1865

Aug   Convention of Gastein gives Holstein to Austria and Schleswig to Prussia. Tension is great between Austria and Prussia.

Oct   In a meeting at Biarritz Bismarck persuades Napoleon III to stay neutral should Prussia go to war with Austria.

1866

June   Prussia annexes Holstein. War breaks out between Prussia and Austria over the future of the Duchies. Many German princes back Austria.

July Austria defeated at Königgrätz.

Aug Prussia annexes Hanover, Schleswig-Holstein, Hesse-Kassel, Nassau and Frankfurt. The North German Confederation is formed made up of Prussia, Oldenburg, Saxony, Mecklenburg, Brunswick, the Thuringian states, part of Hesse Darmstadt, Hamburg, Bremen and Lubeck.

1867

Feb North German Confederation Parliament opens. An imperial *diet* is to be elected to make laws in Berlin. Bismarck is made Chancellor of the Federation.

1870

Sept Following the defeat of France by Prussia, the Rhineland states are brought into the German Confederation.

Nov Württemberg and Bavaria join the North German Confederation.

1871

Jan William I, King of Prussia, becomes Emperor of the new German Reich. Bismark is the first Chancellor.

Liberal Nationalism

It is a commonplace in studies of this period that German liberalism and national awareness underwent a reawakening in the years after 1859. The summer of that year saw events in Italy quickening towards national unification and Napoleon III's diplomatic and military involvement revived old fears from the 1840s of French designs on the Rhine. The immediate consequence was the reorganisation of nationalist forces in the National Association (*Nationalverein*), which led the way in calling for German national unification under the leadership of Prussia. Historians have rightly emphasised the way in which the National Association was closely linked to a range of other organisations – the national congresses of economists, chambers of commerce and lawyers which sprang up at the end of the 1850s, for example. Equally important was the intimate relationship between the Association and the liberal or progressive parties which won rising support in many German states including Prussia in the early 1860s. But, on the whole, historians have seen an essential weakness in this organised liberal nationalism. Although different studies present different views on this point, it would be fair to say that most historians would argue that liberal nationalism succeeded in winning only a limited base of support and that that support came overwhelmingly from urban, propertied groups, with lawyers and other professional groups noticeably over-represented. Such a view is easily comprehensible in view of the fact that at its peak the National Association managed to gain only 25,000 members and that liberal electoral successes were won in states with restrictive franchises and with low levels of electoral participation; for example in the Prussian elections of 1862 and 1863. Moreover, this impression of limited mass support was undoubtedly shared by many liberal nationalists at the time, for all their willingness to make large claims in public about their status as the true representatives of the people. As the liberal nationalist mayor of the north German town of Harburg put it in 1866:

> No member of the national party, if he considers the present circumstances objectively . . . can doubt that his party requires a half century yet to make its views and ideas accepted in all parts of the population and thus to make possible their realisation.

The Prussian elections of 1866, which were held on the same day as the battle of Königgrätz and which saw an enormous swing to the conservatives, were but the first of a sequence of salutary lessons in the limitations of the liberals' ability to engender and retain mass support.

A coalition of interests

There is, however, another side to this story. The events of 1859 generated a considerably more complicated set of political developments than has often been appreciated. There was already a widespread feeling among the statesmen of the German Confederation that the institutional underpinnings of that Confederation were in urgent need of further development. Work had already begun on the preparation of a nationwide code of commercial laws, which was completed in 1861. Fears of French expansionism were by no means restricted to those who would have called themselves liberal in political terms, and there was widespread anxiety about the ability of the Confederation's unwieldy decision-making structure to defend the German states in times of crisis. Politicians and others who were deeply hostile to what they saw as Prussia's expansionist ambitions were rapidly coming to the conclusion that those ambitions were best blocked by a purposeful consolidation of the unity of the Confederation on a national basis. By the early 1860s, there were very few influential voices to be heard arguing that things could go on as they had done up to now. The question that divided German opinion most was not so much whether the German states should develop closer ties with one another. Rather, it was the political form of the new Germany and the related question of the location of sovereignty which lay at the heart of the controversy.

At this point, it is worth remembering that the framework of German politics in the 1860s was essentially local and regional – a fact that has tended to be obscured by the rhetoric of the nation and of 'Germanness', which was central to the arguments of the period. The German states varied greatly in their levels of social and economic development, the religious affiliations of their populations, their administrative and institutional arrangements, all of which structured attitudes to the future of Germany on an essentially local basis. The aversion to Prussia was, as is well known, strong in southern states such as Baden, but was to be found in scarcely less pronounced form in the non-Prussian states of northern Germany as well. Regional tensions existed not just between the German states but within them as well. Virtually all German states in 1866 were new states to the extent that they combined dynastic and old established possessions with newer territories acquired at the Congress of Vienna in the aftermath of the Napoleonic Wars. There is considerable evidence that in many areas of Germany the greatest enthusiasm for national unification was to be found in these newer territories where that enthusiasm was a rejection of the legitimacy of newly-acquired princes. Conversely, the older dynastic territories in states such as Hanover or Hesse-Kassel presented a much greater challenge to the liberal nationalists, one indeed which they never satisfactorily met. For all of these reasons, the political groupings of the period were essentially heterogeneous localised coalitions of people, whose political priorities varied greatly. Put another way, acceptance of an ideology of liberal nationalism meant different things to different people and those differences were basically rooted in local affairs and preconceptions.

The importance of localism

These local and regional roots of political activity were not merely one factor among many that were at work in the 1860s; they were of decisive importance in defining the framework within which aspirant politicians had to operate. As early as the 1840s, liberal nationalists like Heinrich von Gagern – perhaps *the* dominant political figure in the late 1840s – had bemoaned the limitations imposed on political development by the plethora of small states, in which conservative princes and élites retained their dominance. The association of national unification with the ending of the influence of reactionary forces within the states was an important feature of German politics after 1848 as well. Hanoverian politicians like Rudolf von Bennigsen and Johannes Miquel, who were to become influential leaders of the National Liberal Party in 1867, were agreed by 1855 that the domestic political problems of their native Hanover were insoluble without national unification and they were far from being alone in this view. The very frequency of liberal complaints about 'small-stateness' (*Kleinstaaterei*) reveals the dominant role played in their calculations by local political battles and frustrations. If they tended to argue that national unity would lead to freedom, their view of that freedom was very much defined in terms of what they felt was unobtainable in the local conditions of Germany before 1866.

Furthermore, the organisations which sprang up in the late 1850s and early 1860s and which provided much of the underpinning of liberal, nationalist politics tended to exist on an essentially local basis as well. Here, a vital role was played by associations devoted to recreational, ostensibly 'unpolitical' activities such as singing, shooting and gymnastics. Such activities had, to be sure, a history of association with the nationalist cause which went back to the Napoleonic Wars and which caused them to be the frequent objects of suspicion on the part of the public authorities. By the early 1860s, these associations were often linked together into national organisations, which met regularly for annual congresses. Contemporary policemen and subsequent historians have concurred in suspecting these national congresses of sharpshooters, gymnasts and so on of being central to the framework of liberal politics, providing contacts between local liberal or nationalist groups. There are grounds for thinking that such suspicions are correct, but not perhaps in the way in which they have at times been presented. In particular, it should not be imagined that these organisations were merely a seemingly innocuous 'front' for political agitation by the National Association or associated groups.

Social life and sentiment

A characteristic of these recreational associations was that they expressly renounced direct political activity almost everywhere in Germany. Admittedly, such statements were partly motivated by the desire to remain in existence, for overtly political organisations were generally banned by the police after 1848. On the other hand, there is substantial evidence that participants in such organisations welcomed the exclusion of politics from their affairs and there were many cases where attempts to use the clubs for illicit political agitation were rebuffed by the membership. To many gymnasts, singers or sharpshooters, the ability of their clubs to transcend political divisions was a sign of vitality and strength, an expression of the solidarity of the local community without the tensions and divisions which political activity generated. But we should be aware of the limitations inherent in this conception of 'politics'. What was meant here was party politics, for example the taking up of positions on such questions as what type of German nation-state was desirable, whether Prussia should assume the leadership of the national cause at the expense of Austria and so on. An unpolitical stance certainly did not mean ignoring a commitment to the future development of the nation in general terms, and many recreational clubs fervently believed that their avoidance of politics actively contributed to the strength of patriotic sentiment. For all the local variations in Germany, this conception of unpolitical patriotism was perhaps the dominant mode of political expression among educated Germans in the 1860s. Within this patriotism a wide variety of different political views were concealed which only emerged fully in the aftermath of Bismarck's wars of unification. Nationalism was then first and foremost a rhetoric, a mode of discourse with a broad mass appeal. It was the process of converting that appeal into a programme in the world of practical politics, which generated the deep divisions of the late 1860s and 1870s.

This impression is confirmed when two important, though as yet imperfectly understood, aspects of public life in the 1860s are considered. The first of these is the succession of anniversary celebrations, which fell in the years after 1859. The centenaries of the births of the poet Schiller and the philosopher Fichte in 1859 and 1862 respectively both saw widespread festivals in which nationalist sentiments were openly expressed. The contemporary novelist Wilhelm Raabe went so far as to see the Schiller celebrations as the birth of the unity of the German people, and historians have noted the 'national pathos' which attended these festivals. The same could be said, perhaps in increasing measure, of the celebrations of the fiftieth anniversaries of the great victories over Napoleon at the battles of Leipzig and Waterloo. Once again, these anniversaries saw lengthy festivals with strong expressions of the yearning for national unity and strength. In some places, these festivals were organised by members of the National Association, often with the encouragement of the leaders of local urban councils, who helped to fund them. But this was by no means uniformly the case and many speakers at these festivals confined themselves to general statements of enthusiasm for the patriotic cause and avoided overt references to a particular political position. This was for example true of the Schiller celebrations in the poet's native town of Marbach in Württemberg, where one of the principal organisers – himself a noted supporter of the National Association – regarded it as self-evident that he would not use the occasion to promote the Association's views. Such a course would, he believed, have introduced an unnecessarily divisive, sectarian note into what was intended to be a celebration of the patriotic unity of the town.

The Schleswig-Holstein affair

The second major feature of public life was the mounting agitation over the future of Schleswig-Holstein, which came to a head in 1863–4. In many German states, this issue produced by far the greatest level of agitation and mobilisation of opinion that had been seen since 1848. Meetings called to declare support for the claim of the Augustenburg dynasty to the duchies in late 1863 frequently attracted 10,000 or more participants and vast sums of money were raised in that cause. The gymnastics and other recreational associations which were, as we have seen, broadly linked to the nationalist cause were heavily involved, and there is no doubt that the future of Schleswig-Holstein was *the* political issue in the minds of most Germans two years before the Prusso-Austrian war. That this was the case was all the more striking in that the preferred solution of the nationalists – that the reputedly liberal Duke of Augustenburg would inherit the duchies – was never a practical possibility, conflicting as it did with the policy of both Austria and Prussia.

The Schleswig-Holstein affair was a major turning-point in the history of German nationalist politics in the 1860s. As was to be the case later, in 1866 and 1870–71, war forced to the fore the issue which most plagued nationalism: i.e. the form of national unity. It should be remembered that, as part of the broad politics of nationalism, a rival to the National Association had been created in 1862 in the form of the Reform Association (*Reformverein*). This body, whose stated goal was to counteract the influence of the National Association by pressing for a 'large German' solution through reform of the Confederation including Austria, was plagued by internal divisions and incoherences, particularly between the conservative, clericalist and democratic republican groups included within it. Yet, for a time in the early 1860s it managed to attract the support of a far broader section of the population in many German states than the National Association. The reasons for this are complicated but worthy of brief consideration. From one perspective the *großdeutsch* movement was a means of protecting the German princes against the threat of Prussian expansion. From another, it was attractive precisely because it offered a vision of the future which blended the nationalist vision of progress towards unity with the deep-rooted suspicions of centralization of government, which found their origins in the localism of much of German political culture. The *großdeutsch* movement was thus never merely a 'front' for reactionary anti-nationalist interests, however much the National Association may have claimed otherwise.

The existence and (as it turned out transient) popularity of the *großdeutsch* movement provides clear evidence of the breadth of appeal of nationalist rhetoric, which we have already noted. That this was the case was shown clearly by the Schleswig-Holstein agitation. The late summer and autumn of 1863 saw widespread calls for the *großdeutsch* and *kleindeutsch* wings of the nationalist movement to submerge their 'political' differences for the greater good of Germany. This actually happened with the creation of the so-called Committee of 36, which included elements from both wings, to direct the Schleswig-Holstein agitation. Schleswig-Holstein associations sprang up all over Germany, particularly outside East Elbian Prussia, and these local groups likewise incorporated both *kleindeutsch* and *großdeutsch* elements in a common cause. It is difficult to avoid the conclusion that the scale of the Schleswig-Holstein agitation was the product of this ability to subsume what divided Germans most (the form of national unity) into what divided them least – a general commitment to the nation.

This situation was not to last. The refusal of Prussia and Austria to pursue the 'national' (i.e. pro-Augustenburg) policy concerning the duchies cast both *kleindeutsch* and *großdeutsch* wings of the national movement into a decline. It appeared that no amount of agitation could dissuade the largest states in Germany from pursuing their own ends. The National Association sank for a time into torpor, but the effect on the Reform Association was dramatically greater. The fact that Bismarck had patently made the running with regard to the duchies effectively deprived the Reform Association of any realistic hope that Austria might be able to take the lead in the German question in the near future. The organised *großdeutsch* movement then collapsed into a welter of smaller groups with little if any influence on events.

Bismarck's impact on the Nationalists

It is then possible and legitimate to see German nationalism as a genuine mass movement without remotely suggesting that Bismarck's 'revolution from above' was in any sense a 'revolution from below'. There can be no doubt about where the political initiative lay in the events leading up to the wars of 1866 and 1870–71. Those wars, as is well known, produced fundamental re-alignments in German politics creating organised particularist parties in many states outside East Elbian Prussia. Like the Reform Association before them, these parties often incorporated groups across the political spectrum, which were united in opposition to Prussian policy. Unlike the Reform Association, however, their basis was much more closely linked with the single issue of the illegitimacy of

Bismarck's policy in relation to the sovereign rights of the princes. In the changed circumstances after 1866, no alternative vision of a united Germany was developed and particularism rapidly became an essentially negative force in the 1870s. Only in the guise of the newly-created Centre Party, formed to defend Roman Catholic interests as the *Kulturkampf* developed after the Franco-Prussian war, did anti-Bismarckian particularism gain a broader set of priorities. Yet that creation, perhaps more than anything else, showed how much the political mould of the 1860s had been broken.

Kleindeutsch nationalism seemed to fare better, if only because its choice of Prussia as the leading element in the future Germany seemed to have been confirmed by events. Yet for all the jubilation, there were clear signs of unease about Bismarckian politics in 1866–67, and both the Austrian war and the subsequent forced annexations in northern Germany strained the support of the National Association very greatly. The clear evidence of the unpopularity of Bismarck's policies in many areas of Germany caused great misgivings among many *kleindeutsch* nationalists and a few even defected to the particularist cause. Nor did the subsequent history of the National Liberal Party suggest any real unity about how German politics should be conducted, how great the powers of the new central parliament should be, the extent of the constitution and so on. Even among those whose vision of the new Germany had in some way been vindicated, then, the ability of practical political decisions (as opposed to vague nationalist rhetoric) to sow discord was clear. This difficulty was to recur throughout the history of the 1871 empire and beyond.

A skilled manipulator such as Bismarck derived many opportunities from this discord within the nationalist camp and to a certain extent his vision of the possibility of 'instrumentalising' German liberal nationalism may have been justified. Yet, two concluding points are worth making in this connection. First, Bismarck's manipulative skills were directed essentially at political parties at a time when those parties imperfectly represented the range of opinions which constituted the nationalist camp. In many ways, partisan divisions cut through the groups which promoted the national cause in the 1860s and this fact may well be a large part of the explanation for the imperfectly understood phenomenon of the 'unpolitical' German. Second, it is highly unlikely that Bismarck's freedom of manoeuvre would have been anything like as great, had it not been for the rapidly growing dominance of nationalist rhetoric as the basic currency of German political debate.

In this sense, and perhaps only in this sense, German nationalism was a mass movement and it played a decisive role in the framing of Bismarckian power politics.

Michael John is a Fellow of Magdalen College, Oxford.

Andrew Lambert
The Crimean War 1854–56: An Historical Illusion?

The misleading title given to the war that broke out in 1854 between Britain and France and Russia has long hindered understanding both of the nature and strategic objectives of that war and of its effects upon the balance of power in Europe.

The object of this article is to demonstrate that the 'Crimean War' so familiar to twentieth-century students of history has no historical reality; the conflict discussed under that label has been created by misguided and derivative scholarship.[1] The very term 'Crimean War' is a later gloss, one that can be dated back to the 1890s, which developed from a concentration on the most newsworthy events of the war, rather than the intentions of the policymakers. The Crimea never held the central position in strategic decision-making that it has achieved in historical studies. The war did not begin or end in the Crimean Peninsula, it was not decided there, and the end of the sanguinary siege of Sevastopol on 9 September 1855 had little bearing on the Russian decision to accept the allied terms in March 1856. Furthermore the British and French never occupied the city of Sevastopol. Contemporary observers were well aware that the Crimean campaign was only a part of the wider Black Sea theatre, and of the vital linkage with the equally significant Baltic theatre. In so far as allied military pressure had any bearing on Russia's decision to accept terms, that pressure came from the Royal Navy in the Baltic.

The current view

The accepted view of the war can be summarised briefly. Russia, reacting to French pressure on Turkey, made heavy-handed demands which amounted to a marked reduction in the independence of the Sultan in his own dominions. These were rejected by the Turks, which in turn forced Britain to support the Sultan in concert with France. Russia occupied the Danubian Principalities (modern day Romania) to coerce Turkey into accepting her terms. Britain and France sent their fleets to Besika Bay (just outside the Dardanelles) to support Turkey without providing Russia with a cause of war. When Russia refused to leave the Principalities, the western powers moved up to cover Constantinople. The Russian fleet then destroyed a Turkish squadron at Sinope on the southern shore of the Black Sea, forcing the allies to react. The allied ultimatum of 27 March 1854 demanded that Russia withdraw from the Principalities. Allied troops occupied the Gallipoli peninsula, before moving up to Constantinople and then on to Varna (on the coast of modern Bulgaria). Under pressure from Austria the Russian army withdrew from the Principalities without coming into contact with the allies. This secured Turkey's Danube Front, enabling the allies to invade the Crimea in September 1854. After a year-long siege, characterised by the heroism of the troops and the incompetence of their commanders and of the politicians at home, Sevastopol finally fell to an assault on 9 September 1855. Thereafter the war drew to an unsatisfactory close in January 1856, heavily influenced by an Austrian Ultimatum demanding that Russia accept the mild allied terms. The other campaigns, in Asia Minor, the Baltic, the White Sea and the Pacific, were of no significance.

This version of the 'Crimean War' is long overdue for revision. In the absence of any serious study of the formulation of British strategy, existing accounts of the war have fallen back on the Charge of the Light Brigade, Florence Nightingale and the horrors of the Crimean Winter. These were real enough, but had almost no impact on the outcome of the war and serve only to mislead.

The main problem for twentieth-century scholarship has been this narrow view taken of the war. English studies of the war all look back to the monumental eight-volume study by A. W. Kinglake, *The Invasion of the Crimea*. One of the great Victorian prose stylists, Kinglake, never intended his book to be a history of the war, merely an account of the Crimean operation down to the death of Lord Raglan in June 1855, some three months before the fall of Sevastopol. In this he would appear to have been consciously attempting to parallel *The Iliad*, another account of a long siege which ends with the death of the hero, rather than the fall of the city. How he could equate the mild, self-effacing Lord Raglan with Achilles is hard to imagine. Later studies reflect all too closely the impact of this weighty tome, commonly referred to as *Kinglake's Crimean War*.[2] Contemporary accounts, including Kinglake's, along with the correspondence of the men who planned and fought the war, all speak of a 'Russian War', a term which would be rather more useful, if only because it opens out the geography of the conflict.

In order to reconsider the nature and results of the war it is necessary to make a fresh start. Existing publications all accept the 'Crimean War' as outlined above. Having started from the wrong place it should come as little surprise that none have resolved the fundamental issues of why the allies went into the Crimea, why the

Russians accepted terms and what the war demonstrated about British strengths and weaknesses at the mid-point of the nineteenth century. A fresh approach requires a re-examination of the original sources, and of the other major theatre of war, the Baltic.

Pre-war planning

The crisis that foreshadowed the Crimean War became a serious issue for the British government in March 1853, on receipt of the first reports of the mission of Prince Menshikov, the Russian Envoy to Constantinople. The Ministry of Lord Aberdeen, a coalition between the small Peelite Party and the Whig/Liberal Party, was particularly ill-suited to meet the situation. Aberdeen and his fellow Peelites feared and distrusted the new Emperor of France, Louis Napoleon III, while the Whigs considered Tsar Nicholas I to be the personification of repression. As the resolution of the crisis required Britain to stand alongside one or other of these powers the debate was long, and often turbulent. The decision to support France was based more on her inability to overthrow Turkey than any faith in her motives.

In the twelve months before war broke out the First Lord of the Admiralty, the Peelite Sir James Graham, prepared two plans to take the war to Russia, gain the initiative and hopefully create a wider alliance to secure an early victory without a large-scale mobilisation of British forces. In the Black Sea he always looked to destroy Sevastopol, the Russian naval base, either by naval or amphibious attack. The operation was finally carried out largely as he had intended. However, where he envisaged a two week-long grand raid, the problems of allied command and the risks of the undertaking resulted in a year-long siege. In the other major theatre, the Baltic, Graham revived the plan set out by Lord Nelson after the Battle of Copenhagen, to attack the Russian battle-squadron based at Reval in April, before the ice that covers much of the Baltic during the winter had melted far enough to allow the ships to escape, or to be reinforced from the main base at Kronstadt. In the event the Russians withdrew their ships in the autumn of 1853. Graham consulted few of his colleagues in preparing these plans, and the Sevastopol strategy crept into the cabinet's thoughts by a process of osmosis rather than deliberation.

Had these operations been successful the allies would have held complete command of the sea. They would then have been at liberty to attack Russia wherever they pleased, and to encourage other powers to join in and provide more troops to carry the war into Russian provinces, from the Caucasus and Georgia in the South to Finland, Poland and the Baltic States in the North. Austria, Prussia and Sweden would all be invited to join the war. The failure of Graham's ambitious plans and the limited war aims and commitment of the allies ensured that the two German powers stood aloof, while Sweden waited until the war was effectively over before showing her hand.

The allied war aims

After discussions lasting from December 1853 the British, French and Austrians finally agreed on a war aims programme in August 1854. Their terms were set out in the 'Four Points'.

- The Russian guarantee of the Danubian Principalities was to be replaced by a European Guarantee
- The Danube was to be a free river
- The Five Power Treaty of 1841 was to be revised in the interests of the balance of power
- The Christian subjects of the Sultan were to be placed under European and not Russian protection

Russia rejected these terms, but Austria did not join the allies. Austrian interests were well served by armed neutrality. She desired only the reduction of Russian influence in the Danube basin, not the destruction of the conservative order in Europe of which Tsar Nicholas I was the gendarme.[3]

Ultimately Russia was forced to accept the same terms, once more urged on her by the government at Vienna. However, this should not obscure the fact that Austria was never prepared to fight. In November 1855 she sent the final ultimatum to St Petersburg at the very time her army was being demobilised. The diplomatic manoeuvres of the German powers did not end the war. By remaining neutral Austria and Prussia only forced the war into a particular form and restricted it to the geographical fringes of Europe; they did not control its outcome.

Allied strategy

With only the vaguest set of war aims, the allies were always going to face a problem in forming a strategy to secure the nebulous results required by the internal stresses of a coalition ministry and a coalition of nations at war. For this reason Graham was reticent with his designs, while his colleague Lord Palmerston, then Home Secretary, spoke of the widest possible campaigns to reduce Russia to the situation she had occupied at the outset of Catherine the Great's reign. Palmerston had a very clear conception of the long-term interests of Britain: he realised that Russia and the United

States would be the real rivals for British world power once they had harnessed their continental resources and made full use of the technology that Britain pioneered. To sustain British primacy he favoured exploiting the opportunity of 1854, and specifically the French alliance, to inflict a defeat on Russia that would set her back a generation or more. In 1861–63 a similar opportunity beckoned in the New World, but domestic and French support were not available, the real possibility of British intervention in the American Civil War was forestalled, although the vision remained. In fact both Russia and the United States were to suffer such damage that they did not threaten British interests until the end of the nineteenth century.

The decision to attack Sevastopol was the only major strategic decision taken by allied statesmen before the problems of the Crimean campaign began to dictate the direction of the war. Once ashore the allies could not leave until they had beaten the Russians. As a result the wider Black Sea theatre, including support for rebels in Georgia and Circassia and the Turkish Asian front, were given little attention. Essentially the allies elected to open their Black Sea campaign with a major raid. Their failure to carry out the original plan forced them to spend the winter outside Sevastopol, which had never been intended, and exposed the armies to the full rigour of a particularly harsh winter under canvas. When the British, and to a lesser extent, French public became aware of this it became politically imperative to secure an early improvement in the condition of the troops, and some dramatic results to deflect the widespread dissatisfaction with the conduct of the ministers. Lord Aberdeen's government fell in January 1855, to be replaced by many of the same ministers, partly shuffled into new offices, under Lord Palmerston, who was popularly believed to be the one man capable of 'winning' the war. In fact Palmerston's period as war premier proved particularly frustrating. He could not persuade his colleagues to enlarge on the Four Points, to facilitate the aggressive war against Russia that he really desired, and he had to accept an increasing degree of French direction of the war in the Crimea. The first problem reflected the weakness of his political position, the latter the weakness of the British army, which was reduced to raising corps of mercenaries from Switzerland, Germany and Italy to supplement the slow recruitment of domestic troops.

French war aims were never identical to those of Britain. Louis Napoleon desired a quick victory to raise the prestige of his regime, and a European Congress to overthrow the Vienna settlement of 1815 and re-establish France as a dominant force in world politics. As the leader of a military power, who had used the army to seize power in 1851, Louis depended on the support of his generals. In consequence he was only interested in a military success in the Crimea. The French treated British concern over the fate of the Turkish fortress at Kars in Asia Minor, and the support of the Circassian rebels, as merely attempts to protect the routes to India, refusing to lend any support, or even to countenance the movement of the Turkish army in the Crimea to Asia Minor until after the fall of Sevastopol. With a curious irony, the fall of Sevastopol was brought about by a naval campaign that the French twice attempted to cancel.

The fall of Sevastopol

Sevastopol was never surrounded by allied troops, the north side of the harbour was always open, and any number of troops and all types of supplies could be sent in by the main Russian army, which lay inland near Simpheropol. Whenever the allies pressed hard on Sevastopol the Russian field army would move onto the allied flank, at Balaclava and then Inkerman in late 1854, to force the British and French to stop the siege. This link between the Russian army and the fortress had been created by Prince Menshikov, the Russian Commander-in-Chief, who has generally been considered very unsatisfactory. Yet for nine months his strategy effectively kept the allies out of Sevastopol, and forced them to fight a campaign of attrition at the end of supply lines 3,000 miles long. Only the availability of steam shipping enabled the British and to a lesser extent the French to hang on through the severe winter, and then to build up a force of men and artillery that could win this battle. However, before any decisive moves could be made the allies had to break the link between the Russian field army and the city. Louis Napoleon and the French high command proposed taking the field to surround the city, but the allies never had sufficient troops to carry out such a plan.

Realising that the campaign had become a contest of strength rather than skill the British, particularly Sir James Graham, advocated an attack on Russian logistics. By occupying the Sea of Azov with a squadron of gunboats in May 1855 the British effectively cut off the Russian army from its main supply base in the basin of the River Don. Road transport, still drawn by horses and bullocks, could not replace the loss of water transport across the Sea of Azov, and the Russian army was forced to relinquish the defence of Sevastopol. In August the Russians staged a desperate frontal assault on strong allied defences, and only weeks later abandoned the city, after standing one last assault. However, having retreated across Sevastopol harbour they used the high northern shore to erect batteries that dominated the city, and prevented the allies from occupying it in safety. For the remainder of the war the two armies sat and watched one another across a deep moat, too exhausted and cautious to move.

Once Sevastopol had fallen allied attention switched to the wider theatre. The British were worried, with good cause in the event, for the Turkish-Asian border fortress of Kars, which surrendered on 23 November. Palmerston and others wanted to move the British army to Asia Minor in 1856, the French preferred to operate around Odessa. On 17 October 1855 an Anglo-French amphibious taskforce captured the Fortress at Kinburn, which covered the entrance to the River Bug, Russia's main transport route from the interior, and the site of her main shipyard, at Nicolaiev some 20 miles from the sea. The operation was noteworthy for the first use in combat of armour-plated warships, but was not followed up. After that the Black Sea theatre became quiet, the allies used the winter to ponder on their strategy, the Russians to reflect on the logistic and sanitary disaster that was rapidly reducing their army to a series of full hospitals and large burial details.

The Baltic Theatre

If there is any single aspect of the 'Crimean War' that stands in need of revision it is the importance of the Baltic Campaigns. Paul Kennedy was merely following a long line of scholars when he dismissed them as 'never very serious', in his latest book.[4] Sir James Graham's pre-war hopes for the Baltic were disappointed in March 1854 since there were no Russian ships at Reval, and the Swedish government was not interested in joining the allies. These two events were decisive for 1854, because the powerful British fleet of large battleships and cruisers did not have a single small gunboat or mortar vessel to carry the war to the Russian forts and harbours, and had no troops for amphibious operations. Graham had depended on Sweden for these resources. Without them he was forced to accept a French army, which was used to capture the fortress of Bomarsund in the Aland Islands, midway between Sweden and Russian Finland. To avoid the well-deserved criticism that should have been made of his policy Graham made a scapegoat of the Admiral Commanding the Fleet, Sir Charles Napier, at the time he was building the very gunboats and mortar vessels he had refused to prepare earlier in the year, when Napier requested them.

In August 1855, while all attention was turned to Sevastopol, the Baltic fleet used its gunboats and mortar vessels to destroy the Russian dockyard at Sweaborg (outside modern Helsinki). This success, added to that at Kinburn in October, pointed the way

forward for the British government. With France increasingly looking for an early compromise peace, Palmerston had to find a major
strategic move for early 1856 that would force Russia to concede his
terms. Unable to rely on France, and lacking anything like the
necessary number of troops for a military solution, he fell back,
unwillingly, on the naval plan. In both Baltic campaigns an outstanding Naval Officer, Captain Bartholomew Sulivan had directed
all the major operations, and minutely examined the Russian defences. He proposed using a large force of armoured batteries,
mortar vessels and gunboats supported by rocket firing boats, the
regular fleet and a large force of Royal Marines to bombard and
capture the main Russian naval base at Kronstadt. Kronstadt was
also the seaward defence of St Petersburg; if Kronstadt were
captured the Russian capital would be open to allied attack. To
carry out the attack, without the aid of France, the Royal Navy
prepared the 'Great Armament of 1856' a force of 250 steam
gunboats, 100 mortar vessels, 10 armoured batteries and numerous
supporting craft to be ready for operations in April 1856. Only
Britain had the industrial and financial strength required to carry
out this programme in such a short space of time.

Why Russia accepted the allied terms

In January 1856 the Russian Council of Ministers discussed the
Austrian Ultimatum, which they realised was a mere gesture while
the Austrian Army was in process of demobilising. They saw no
real danger in the Black Sea theatre, but were very concerned by
developments closer to home. The Russian economy had collapsed
under the pressure of a strict British blockade. The only real friend
left to the Russians, Prussia, was now urging them to accept terms,
while Sweden had aligned herself with the allies in return for a
guarantee of her territorial integrity and it was rumoured that she
was now committed to joining the war. However, the catalyst for a
year of disasters would be the capture of Kronstadt. After the fall of
Sevastopol the great engineer General Totleben had been recalled
to work on the island fortress and every effort was in progress.
However, the technological superiority and boundless confidence
of the Royal Navy gave them an edge that should have proved
decisive. Rather than take the risk of defeat Russia accepted the
humiliation of allied terms. In consequence the 'Great Armament'
never reached the Baltic, let alone attacked Kronstadt.

The impact of the war

One area where existing accounts are particularly faulty is in their
appreciation of the long-term consequences of the 'Crimean War'.

The defeat suffered by Russia forced her to abandon her dominant influence in central Europe. Within 15 years Prussia had used the power vacuum to create a unified Germany, and until the Red Army destroyed the Third Reich in 1945 Russia never recovered the position of 1853. Prince Albert celebrated the removal of Russian influence from Germany as the one great result of the war, George V and Kaiser Wilhelm II might well have reflected on the truth of that in the years after 1918. The war also highlighted the internal weakness of Russia. Economically backward, with almost all capital tied up in land and the labour force tied into the soil, it was impossible to create new industries, or raise fresh armies. The same Crown Council meeting that accepted the allied terms in January 1856 also agreed to the abolition of the status of serf. While it required another seven years to implement this decision it should be stressed that its origins lay in war and defeat, not liberal humanity.

The Great Armament for 1856 assembled at Spithead as the Peace Conference began to deliberate in Paris. The sheer size of the force was used by the British diplomats to silence any attempt by Russia to evade the allied terms. Influential neutrals were encouraged to inspect these mighty preparations, and reports were doubtless soon available in St Petersburg. Once the war was officially over the Baltic Fleet staged a triumphal Review, suitably enough on St George's Day 1856. The warning should have been clear to every major nation of the world. The Royal Navy had the power to destroy any naval arsenal and the fleet that sheltered inside. British seapower had reached its very zenith, unrivalled in strength, technical skill and experience. When Britain and Russia next came close to blows over Turkey, in 1877–79, Russia backed down. One British fleet lay off Constantinople, another was assembled at home for a campaign in the Baltic. British seapower was never the passive, defensive asset portrayed by twentieth-century commentators looking for the earliest possible period from which to date Britain's Imperial decline. By contrast it remained unrivalled as a sea control force and a means of amphibious power projection until the early years of the Second World War.

Notes

(1) For a full-length study of these issues see: Lambert, A.D. *The Crimean War: British Grand Strategy Against Russia, 1853–56* (1990).
(2) Kinglake, A.W. *The Invasion of the Crimea* (1863–69) 8 vols.
(3) Schroder, P.W. *Austria, Great Britain and the Crimean War: The Destruction of the European Concert.* Ithaca (1972).
(4) Kennedy, P.M. *The Rise and Fall of the Great Powers* (1988) p.173.

Further Reading

Curtiss, J.S. *Russia's Crimean War* (1979).
Echard, W.E. *Napoleon III and the Concert of Europe* (1983).
Rich, N. *Why the Crimean War?* (1985).
Saab, A.P. *The Origins of the Crimean Alliance* (1977).

Andrew Lambert is based at the Department of War Studies, King's College, London.

James McMillan
Idealist or Opportunist?
Reassessing Napoleon III

James McMillan suggests that Napoleon III was neither the liberal nor the despot of historical controversy, but a political fixer riding his luck through difficult circumstances.

Historians, like contemporaries, have been deeply divided over what to make of Napoleon III, the man who came from nowhere to become President of the Second French Republic in December 1848 and then Emperor of the Second French Empire in December 1852. His story has been told many times, but the emperor remains something of an enigma and his aims and achievements controversial. Some historians are not even convinced that he was who he purported to be: the nephew of Napoleon I. Marital difficulties between Napoleon's brother Louis, King of Holland, and his wife Hortense Beauharnais have been invoked to suggest that the son who was born to the couple in Paris on 20 April 1808 and given the name of Charles Louis Napoleon Bonaparte may have been only a Beauharnais rather than a Bonaparte.[1] Throughout his life, Louis Napoleon remained a puzzle. It was said of him that he spoke five languages and that he knew how to be silent in all of them. The Austrian ambassador Metternich called him the Sphinx of the Tuileries, though Bismarck, less impressed, claimed that he was a sphinx without a secret.

One point of the present article is to show how the considerable divergence of historical opinion over the career of Napoleon III tends to throw light less on the man and the statesman than on the assumptions, predilections and ideological positions of the authors writing about him. Bias is always a problem in historical writing, but in the case of Napoleon III it is excessive. Biographies of the emperor and studies of the empire are always reinterpretations, or re-inventions. Secondly, the article suggests that, rather than perpetuating the debate as to whether Napoleon III was a 'goodie' or a 'baddie', historians could usefully adopt a less *engagé* approach to the study of his reign.

Black Legend

In France, Napoleon III was long represented in the tradition of the 'Black Legend'. Essentially the creation of his republican political

Main Events in the Life of Napoleon III

1808	Born Charles Louis Napoleon Bonaparte
1836	Tries, unsuccessfully, to depose the July Monarchy
1840	Tries again to remove Louis Philippe. Captured and imprisoned at Ham. Spends his time in prison writing treatises.
1846	Escapes from prison and flees to London
1848	Elected President of the Second Republic
1851	Louis Napoleon seizes power in a *coup d'état*; a new constitution is approved in a plebiscite
1852	Second Empire established on 2 December, becomes Napoleon III.
1854	France sides with Britain during the Crimean War
1856	Paris Peace Conference concludes the war.
1858	Attempt on Louis Napoleon's life by Felice Orsini; Orsini arrested and executed. The Compact of Plombières. Napoleon III agrees with Cavour to help expel the Austrians from Italy in return for receiving Savoy and Nice.
1859	Truce of Villafranca made with the Austrians
1861	Napoleon III establishes a Catholic Empire in Mexico. Makes Maximilian of Austria the Emperor. Maximilian shot by Mexicans in 1867.
1870	France routed by Prussia and forced to surrender at Sedan.
1871	Treaty of Frankfurt imposes harsh penalties on the French, including the loss of Alsace-Lorraine.
1873	Louis Napoleon dies in exile in England.

opponents, it was fabricated by prominent writers such as Victor Hugo, who dubbed the emperor 'Napoleon the Little', and by artists like Daumier, who created the cynical and devious cartoon character 'Ratapoil' to personify the empire. For republicans, Napoleon III was an usurper who substituted an oppressive authoritarian regime for a democratic republic and compounded this crime by leading the country into the shame and disaster of humiliating defeat in the Franco-Prussian war of 1870. Under the Third Republic, the republican view assumed a less polemical and more 'scientific' guise at the hands of professional historians writing and teaching at the Sorbonne. Socialist historians further refined the republican line, denying that there was ever any progressive side to the Second Empire or that workers were ever taken in by Napoleon III's claim to be their friend.[2]

French conservatives produced their own variation on the 'Black

Legend' theme. For the upper classes (*grands notables*) who had been in power under the July Monarchy, the 1848 revolution had been an even bigger trauma than the re-establishment of the empire, and indeed they had been prepared to rally to Louis Napoleon's *coup d'état* in 1851 and the re-establishment of the empire in 1852, out of fear of a 'Red' republican takeover. Yet they were reluctant imperialists, and in Pierre de la Gorce they found a historian who expressed their ambivalence about Napoleon III and his regime. De la Gorce portrayed the emperor as personally sympathetic – humane, well-intentioned and fundamentally decent – but too much of a dreamer, utopian, conspirator and gambler. His regime was a disaster, partly because of his own personal defects, but even more because in the place of classic parliamentary liberalism it could offer only either demagogy derived from its revolutionary origins or hard-faced reaction as advocated to the emperor by evil counsellors such as Rouher.[3] De la Gorce's assessment of Napoleon III, it is worth noting, was largely recreated for the benefit of Anglophone readers in the 1950s and 1960s by the English historians J.M. Thompson and J.P.T. Bury.[4]

Outside France the 'Black Legend' was further refined and brought up to date by other British and American historians. In Britain, in the early years of the twentieth century, Liberals like H.A.L. Fisher and G.P. Gooch remained hostile towards the essentially 'authoritarian' empire.[5] More dramatically, after the Second World War, others saw in Napoleon III a precursor of fascism and the founder of a police state – the 'first mountebank dictator', in the words of Sir Lewis Namier.[6] Popularised by the likes of L.C.B. Seaman, this was a particularly far-fetched view, since the Second Empire was no more of a police state than the Second or Third Republics.

'Good' Napoleon III

The 'Black Legend' did not go uncontested. In France, the case for the defence was put at massive length by Emile Ollivier in his multi-volume history of the regime produced between 1895 and 1918.[7] A republican who had been won over to the Second Empire by the liberal reforms of the 1860s, Ollivier was effectively the 'Prime Minister' of the Liberal Empire at its inauguration in January 1870. His work was written as a defence of the statesmanship of both himself and his imperial master. In his pages, Napoleon III emerges as a far-sighted and progressive leader, a man of vision, who, like Ollivier himself, was a product of the spirit of 1848 – generous, idealistic and keen to reconcile the thirst for liberty and democracy with the principle of order. The Liberal Empire itself was a great experiment and could have been a marvellous success, had it not been for the tragic circumstances which produced the war of 1870 and its disastrous outcome. Napoleon III was simply unlucky, a victim of the machinations of opponents at home and abroad (above all, of Bismarck).

Ollivier's account can hardly be regarded as objective history, being primarily a personal apologia. It had little impact on historical opinion in France. In the Anglo-American world, however, it served as the basis for revisionist views of the emperor and his regime which came to establish themselves as a new orthodoxy in the place of the 'Black Legend'. The Cambridge historian, F.A. Simpson, argued that the Second Empire was historically more important than the First, since it shattered the Vienna settlement and for a time restored French preponderance in Europe. Moreover, as the champion of the principle of nationality, Napoleon III had a significant input to the reshaping of mid-nineteenth-century Europe.[8] Subsequently, a whole series of studies of Napoleon III appeared, explicitly taking issue with the 'Black Legend' and presenting him as a much-maligned historical figure in need of rehabilitation – the outstanding statesman of his time, a visionary and a progressive.[9]

In revisionist re-inventions of Napoleon III, a consistent theme is that of the modernity of the man and his regime. Theodore Zeldin has portrayed him as the statesman who brought political modernity to France, breaking the mould of French politics by weakening the power of the *notables*.[10] Studies of Napoleon III's foreign policy see him as a 'good European'. Already in the 1930s some historians saw him not as the harbinger of fascism but as a precursor of the League of Nations.[11] More recently, a study which emphasises the importance he attached to congress diplomacy and attempts to establish a European confederation presents a Napoleon III who could be a forerunner of Jacques Delors.[12] In studies of the economic and social policies of the Second Empire, however, it is a more Gaullist image of the emperor which emerges – as the advocate of economic progress and a close partnership between the state and industry, he has been hailed as a pioneer of the technocracy characteristic of the Fifth Republic.[13] In all of these incarnations, Napoleon III appears to have been reinvented mainly in accordance with changing political and ideological climates. Whether they take us any closer to the truth about the Second Empire must remain a moot point.

The question of power

In order to reassess Napoleon III and the Second Empire, what is required is less emphasis on ideologically-inspired precedents and parallels and more attention to the central question of personal power in a personalist regime. Napoleon III knew what he wanted. In his *Napoleonic Ideas* of 1839 he set out a programme which envisaged strong executive government, an end to revolution through the satisfaction of the legitimate aspirations of the masses, the pursuit of social and economic modernity and the revision of the Vienna settlement in order to reshape Europe in line with the 'principle of nationalities'. He found, however, that he was rarely able to achieve his goals, either at home or abroad, and that often his actions had consequences far from those which he had intended.

Superficially, Napoleon III appeared to be in a very strong position and it would certainly be a mistake to underestimate the regime's capacity for repression, particularly in the 1850s. The very creation of the empire derived from Louis Napoleon's willingness to stage a ruthless *coup d'état* against the republic whose constitution he had sworn to uphold, and throughout the 1850s the police continued to crack down hard on Republican opponents. In 1858, after the attempt on his life by the Italian conspirator Orsini, Napoleon III unleashed a reign of terror against those whom he regarded as the fomenters of discord. Martial law was introduced and a Law of General Security permitted large numbers of arbitrary arrests and deportations. Nevertheless, the emperor discovered that there were limits to his power even under the so-called 'authoritarian empire'.

His problem was that, in order to have his policies implemented, he depended on the good will of many individuals who did not share his aims and ambitions. Not even his ministers could be completely relied upon to translate his 'Napoleonic ideas' into effective actions. Few were genuine Bonapartists, but rather products of the world of Orleanism with many links with the *grands notables*. Morny, the emperor's half-brother, was the epitome of the regime's connections with big business. Only Persigny, Minister of the Interior and long-time comrade from the conspiratorial days of his youth, was completely devoted to the emperor, since even other members of the imperial family, such as his cousin Prince Jerome Napoleon ('Plon-Plon') and Walewski, the illegitimate son of Napoleon I, disagreed with him on important points of policy. Hence the celebrated quip attributed to Napoleon III: 'What a government is mine! The empress is a legitimist: Napoleon-Jerome a republican: Morny Orleanist, I myself am a socialist. The only Bonapartist is Persigny and he is mad!'

Like his ministers, members of the Legislative Body also tended to come from an Orleanist background and had rallied to the empire out of social fear rather than from any genuine enthusiasm for

Bonapartism, even if they were elected as 'official' candidates. Once the 'red menace' receded, they were tempted to push for the reintroduction of a more liberal and parliamentary form of government, and refused to allow themselves to be used simply as a rubber stamp for authoritarianism. Nor could Napoleon III count on the bureaucracy as an instrument of direct administrative rule. The *Conseil d'Etat*, staffed yet again by members of the former élite, frequently blocked legislation desired by the emperor. The prefects were a less homogeneous body, but only a minority were dedicated to the implementation of 'Napoleonic ideas'. Most found themselves having to tread warily so as not to antagonise the local élites in their departments. In the absence of a Bonapartist party (which Napoleon III refused to create so as to appear a truly 'national' rather than a party leader), the emperor's power was inevitably limited by his need to propitiate the old ruling classes – their acceptance of his regime was at best grudging. Likewise, the goodwill of church leaders was conditional, and forfeited once Napoleon III began to show more sympathy for the cause of Italian nationalism than for the papacy.

Foreign policy

As at home, so abroad Napoleon III was conscious of limitations on his power and freedom for manoeuvre. He dreamed of a Europe united on the basis of peoples and nationalities, rather than held together by a 'Holy Alliance' of monarchs. He also envisaged a greater European confederation in which popular aspirations to national unification would be realised and through which peace on the continent would be preserved by means of international co-operation between the larger nation-states. But, quite apart from the fact that Napoleon III was not so single-minded as to make the *politique des nationalités* the only goal of his foreign policy (in an age of *Realpolitik* he was one of its foremost practitioners, and purely national and dynastic objectives were rarely far from his thoughts), the emperor was always aware that he could not impose himself unilaterally on the international scene. Even after his successes in the Crimean War and the Treaty of Paris he realised he had to proceed warily, trying, as always, to retain the goodwill of Britain (so as to avoid what he regarded as the one great error of his uncle) but also making overtures towards the defeated and resentful Russians. Even at the peak of his influence in international affairs, French power and influence depended very much on the attitude of the other Great Powers. And, after 1863, French pretensions to the mastery of Europe were to be cruelly undermined by Bismarck and Prussia.

Political operator

Napoleon III was not completely the master of France. Still less was he the arbiter of Europe. Traditionally, the reign has been represented as being divided into two phases, one 'authoritarian', the other 'liberal'. In reality, the 'Liberal Empire' was established only right at the end of the reign, in January 1870. Throughout his time in power, Napoleon III presided over a regime which, however much it evolved, was characterised primarily by continuity. He ruled neither as a reactionary, wedded to the defence of the status quo, nor as an orthodox liberal, bent on restoring a parliamentary regime. Rather, he was a *politique*, a political operator who for 18 years – a long time in politics – worked hard at maintaining the political initiative. Until the final calamity of 1870, he can be accounted a shrewd practitioner of the politics of survival who, despite all the obstacles in his way, attempted to carry out an original policy. He was a lonely figure, exercising power through agents who did not share his vision of the future. Instinctively an idealist, he was of necessity an opportunist, struggling to perpetuate his dynasty and to mould events in the image of his convictions. The going, however, was always tough. As he explained to his son, the Prince Imperial, in his Last Will and Testament: 'Power is a heavy burden. You cannot always do the good you would like to do, and your contemporaries are seldom fair.'

These words suggest that, perhaps more than most statesmen, Napoleon III was acutely aware of the ironies of power. If a parallel must be found in modern times, perhaps the best comparison is with another statesman who was in favour of restructuring (*perestroika*) at home and *détente* (*glasnost*) abroad, but who found to his cost that his reforms did not quite work out the way he had intended. It could just be that the most apt reinvention of Napoleon III might be as a proto-Mikhail Gorbachev.

Notes

(1) This has been suggested most recently in Bierman, J. *Napoleon III and His Carnival Empire* (John Murray, 1989).

(2) The best treatment of the historiography is Campbell, S.L. *The Second Empire Revisited: a Study in French Historiography* (Rutgers, 1978).

(3) Gorce, P. de la *Napoléon III et sa politique* (1933).

(4) Thompson, J.M. *Louis Napoleon and the Second Empire* (Blackwell, 1954). Bury, J.P.T. *Napoleon III and the Second Empire* (English Universities Press, 1964).

(5) Fisher, H.A.L. *Bonapartism* (Oxford University Press, 1914). Gooch, G.P. *The Second Empire* (Longman, 1960).

(6) Namier, L. *Vanished Supremacies* (Harper, 1963). pp. 54–64. Compare

Schapiro, J.S. *Liberalism and the Challenge of Fascism* (McGraw-Hill, 1949) pp. 320–31 and Seaman, L.C.B. *From Vienna to Versailles* (Methuen, 1956).

(7) Ollivier, E. *L'Empire libéral: études, récits, souvenirs* 17 vols (1895–1918).

(8) Simpson, F.A. (3rd edn) *The Rise of Louis Napoleon* (Longman, 1951). and Simpson, F.A. (3rd edn) *The Recovery of France* (Longman, 1960).

(9) Compare Corley, T.A.B. *Democratic Despot: a Life of Napoleon III* (Barrie and Rockcliff, 1961) and Smith, W.H.C. *Napoleon III* (Weyland, 1972).

(10) Zeldin, T. *The Political System of Napoleon III* (Macmillan, 1958).

(11) Sencourt, R. *The Modern Emperor* (Appleton-Century, 1933).

(12) Echard, W.E. *Napoleon III and the Concert of Europe* (Louisiana State University Press, 1983).

(13) Dansette, A. *Histoire du Second Empire, Naissance de la France moderne* (1961–76).

James McMillan is Professor of European History at the University of Strathclyde. He is the author of *Napoleon III* in the Longman *Profiles in Power* Series.

Patrick Condren
Examiner's Report

Document questions are an increasingly important part of the A-level syllabus. This report draws attention to the particular skills required in handling them.

Many A-level syllabuses contain document questions. In some ways a document question can seem less daunting, especially perhaps to weaker candidates, than an essay question with its inevitable requirement to work out what is being asked for and need to construct a plausible and effective answer. How much more helpful a document question seems to be, with its subdivided structured questions.

Although there is some truth in this, all students will know that there is nothing to be gained by taking a document less seriously than an essay. Preparation must be just as thorough, concentration and attention to detail just as great. Dealing with real historical material such as documents is one of the fundamental tasks of the historian, and although at A-level such documents appear in a pre-packaged form, the skills needed to make proper use of them are indispensable.

There are some basic techniques which will enable you to make the best of your knowledge and skills. First of all, read the question. If you are taking an exam make doubly sure that you have checked which topic is under discussion. What dates are mentioned? Are you sure you can do well on this topic or period? If not, do you have a better alternative? As you read through the various extracts, make sure that you register who it was that made the comment, and what position he or she held at the time. You need to note whether the extract was from a letter, memoir, diary, official document, public speech etc. It is clearly very important to know to whom the various comments were being addressed. It is just as vital to note precisely when the extracts date from. The timing could make all the difference to your understanding (or not) of a question. There is a natural tendency to neglect such details in the interests of speed, and yet the skills being tested in document questions obviously require the candidate to be aware of bias, differences of opinion, the sequence of events, as well as the wider historical context.

Answering the questions

Of course, if you don't know the material, you will not be able to demonstrate your historical skills to any great effect. As with essay questions, it is vital that you do what you are asked. If you are asked to compare documents, this is what you must do, but in doing this make sure you actually refer to the particular extracts, either by a short quotation, or by a line reference (or both). Don't give in to the temptation to make assumptions based on your own knowledge as you are being asked to handle the extracts which the examiner, or your teacher, has gone to the trouble of assembling. However, if you get a question which asks you to refer to your wider studies, this is what you must do.

Some questions will ask you to assess the reliability or impartiality of a particular extract. When doing this, think hard about who is speaking or writing. Did he or she have an axe to grind at the time? Were they trying to be objective, or were they just giving their own opinion? Do you know what their political views were? Did they belong to a particular political party or social group? Were they in office at the time of writing etc.?

Other questions might ask you to assess the value of a document to the historian. You must think how the extract might clarify an issue, how it could give the reader an insight into the thinking of a person or government, or how it shows the techniques of an orator striving to seduce a crowd. Don't forget that just because the document in question is a tissue of lies it does not necessarily lose its usefulness to a historian of the period who is likely to be delighted to find such a perfect example of someone's dishonesty. As an historian, you should be especially careful not to believe everything you read, but that doesn't mean that you can't use material which shows evidence of being untrue, distorted or biased.

Another point worth making, especially with European sources, is that very often the extracts are translations, and maybe this could account for a particular passage reading awkwardly. You are naturally not in a position to check the accuracy of a translation during an exam, if at all, but there may be some credit to be had for mentioning this if appropriate. This leads on to the problem of language in general. The style of English in use in the nineteenth century was not dramatically different from that of today, but there may be the odd turn of phrase that seems confusing unless you devote time to working out its precise meaning. Further complications can be caused by the kind of terminology used by Marxists or fascists. Stalin's writing and speaking are good examples of this. Never a very gripping read, some of his statements, larded with the curious terminology of Marxism-Leninism, can seem pretty impenetrable. Mussolini also had something of a tendency to make wild and confusing statements, especially in public, though even on paper he was often no clearer. Whatever the difficulties, you must make sure you get the meaning clear in your mind before you start trying to construct answers. Working out your own paraphrased version might help with particularly awkward extracts.

Some examples of documents, questions, and students' answers follow. The topics are from nineteenth-century European history. I have added comments which are intended to be helpful.

Document 1

Austria and France 1859–62.

He sees nothing wrong at all; he has his own comforts, good cooking, cards after dinner – he invited me to dine, but I excused myself and went back to my splendid soldiers in their bivouacs – this Headquarters turns the stomach and I could weep . . . . The poor 9 Corps belongs this morning to the First Army, tomorrow to the Second, and gets its orders from both, which cross each other and contradict each other; so today it marches east, tomorrow west, wearing itself out to no purpose.

(Count Crenneville to his wife, describing a visit to the headquarters of the Austrian Field Marshal Gyulai soon after the Battle of Magenta, 8 June 1859)

Question

How confident can you be of the impartiality of the evidence provided in this document?

Student's answer

> It is a fact that the Austrians were defeated at Magenta by Napoleon III, so it is right to assume that the evidence in the document is impartial because it explains why the Austrians were defeated.

This answer does not really address the problem of partiality. Assuming that we know very little about Crenneville we cannot speak with any confidence of his personality or motives. He was obviously angry about the defeat, and the incompetence, as he saw it, at headquarters, and this may have clouded his judgement somewhat, but given that the letter is to his wife, his criticisms were presumably for private consumption, and not part of any career infighting. Of course, it could be that the countess has good connections at the Imperial court, and that Crenneville knows that in a short time his stories of Gyulai's incompetence will reach the highest level, thus removing a hated rival from his position, and advancing Crenneville's own career! Maybe Crenneville wrote similar letters to dozens of people. But we are in no position to give way to such flights of fancy. What we can say is that: a) The Austrians were defeated; b) Other sources support the view that there were shortcomings in the Austrian handling of the campaign in North Italy; c) Crenneville sounds like a competent commander and a patriotic Austrian, who keeps his critical comments about Gyulai to a letter to his wife. Bearing all this in mind we can thus be fairly confident that the evidence is impartial enough to be relied on.

Document 2

The Making of the German Empire.

In the palace of Louis XIV, in that ancient centre of a hostile power which for centuries has striven to divide and humiliate Germany, the solemn proclamation of the German Empire was made on January 18th . . . . Though the German people, owing to the necessities of the times, were represented at the ceremony only by the German army, the eyes of the entire nation were gratefully turned to the palace where, surrounded by sovereigns, generals, and soldiers, King William announced to the world the assumption by himself and his heirs of a title for the re-establishment of which we have been yearning during the sixty long years it has been in abeyance . . . .

(Germany's) destiny is to add to its power not by conquest but by promoting culture, liberty, and civilisation. As far as the German people are concerned, there will be no more wars in Europe after the determination of the present campaign . . . .

Count Bismarck, having read the King's proclamation to the German nation, the grand duke of Baden stepped forth and exclaimed, 'Long Live his Majesty the Emperor!' The cheers of the assembly were taken up by the bands playing the national anthem.

(An official account, published in Berlin, 24 January 1871)

Question

Discuss what evidence of German nationalism is contained in this document.

Student's answer

This extract is from an official account of the proclamation of the German Empire in 1871. As such it can be expected to give the government line on the events, with particular emphasis on the version of German nationalism favoured by Bismarck. Thus the extract is peppered with references to Germany, the people, the nation and to the tremendous enthusiasm apparent at Versailles. There are naturally no references to the fact that the German 'people' had no significant influence on events, nor to the fact that parts of the 'nation' had been annexed earlier and that there had been considerable reluctance on the part of other 'German' rulers to lose their independence by joining the German Empire. As many liberal German national- ists were soon to discover after the euphoria of victory had faded, the Empire was not the liberal parliamentary state of which they had once dreamed. The crude distortion of history in the first two lines is typical of the whole extract in that it reflects the politically and socially conservative version of German nationalism which Bismarck and his supporters were trying to sell to the recently 'unified' Germany.

It is hard to fault this answer. The question itself carried four marks. Perhaps in showing that there was more than one strand of German nationalism the student has given too full an answer, but there will be no penalty for this, especially with a response of this quality.

Document 3

Italian Unification 1867–1870.

I do hope that Garibaldi will not succeed in starting a movement (against Rome). For at the moment it would probably be repressed . . .; if it succeeded, Rattazzi would take over control . . . and Rome would then find itself ruled by a small-time and immoral politician . . . . If Rome cannot be made the holy city of our Italian nation, it had better remain a ruin (but) one day the flag of the Italian Republic will fly (there) . . . Garibaldi might do it . . . . He loves Rome . . . but looks at the matter more from a materialistic than from a moral point of view . . . Garibaldi is a brave person, noble, good, a man of integrity . . . but there is something lacking.

(Mazzini in a letter, August 1867)

Question

How do the content and style of the document suggest that Mazzini was both a patriot and an idealist?

Student's answer

Mazzini is obviously a patriot because he hopes that one day the Italian flag will fly there (sic). He also seems to approve of Garibaldi who was another Italian patriot. He was an idealist because he had devoted his life to Italian unification.

This is a sloppy and inadequate answer. To do full justice to the question some clear reference must be made to the document. For example, Mazzini calls Rome the 'holy city of our Italian nation' which is a clear proof of how much of a patriot he was. He is also yearning for the day when Rome will become the capital of Italy. That he was also an idealist is made clear by his high moral tone eg. he refers to Rattazzi as an 'immoral politician' and speaks of Garibaldi as being 'noble, good, a man of integrity'. In addition

121

his reference to the 'Italian Republic' shows that in the face of the reality of the monarchical Italy of 1867, he is still hoping for the creation of the republic of which he dreamed in his younger days.

Conclusion

As is to be expected, the answers show various degrees of competence, but there is no reason why with a little more thought and practice the weakest of the students could not improve performance significantly. To summarise, one could conclude with five short questions to be asked when tackling a document question. Who wrote it? To whom was it written? When was it written? Under what circumstances was it written? Why was it written? The answers are up to you.

Patrick Condren teaches History at Eltham College.

Chronology of Events 1815–1870

1815   Napoleon defeated at Waterloo (18 June); exiled to St Helena (26 September)
1818   Congress of Aix-la-Chapelle
1819   Karlsbad Decrees
        The start of the German Zollverein
1820   Revolutions in Spain, Naples and Portugal
        Congress of Troppau
1821   Start of the Greek War of Independence
1822   Castlereagh replaced by Canning as British Foreign Secretary
        Congress of Verona
1823   Monroe doctrine
1824   Death of Louis XVIII; succeeded by Charles X
1825   Canning recognised the independence of the Spanish colonies
        Death of Alexander I of Russia; succeeded by Nicholas I
1827   Death of Canning
        Battle of Navarino
1829   Treaty of Adrianople
1830   July Revolution in France; accession of Louis Philippe
1831   Leopold of Saxe-Coburg became King of the Belgians
1833   Treaty of Unkiar Skelessi
1848   Revolution in Paris; abdication of Louis Philippe
        Second Republic of France proclaimed
        Revolutions in Germany, Hungary and Bohemia
        Louis Napoleon elected President of the French Republic
1849   Rising in Hungary suppressed
1851   *Coup d'état* of Louis Napoleon
1852   Cavour became Prime Minister of Piedmont
        Louis Napoleon, Emperor of the French (Napoleon III)
1854   Outbreak of the Crimean War
1855   Death of Tsar Nicholas I; accession of Alexander II
        Fall of Sevastopol
1856   Peace of Paris
1858   Napoleon III met Cavour at Plombières
1859   Truce of Villafranca
        Battle of Solferino
1860   Savoy and Nice annexed by France
        Sicily and Naples taken by Garibaldi
1861   Victor Emmanuel II, the first king of the Kingdom of Italy
1861   French Expedition to Mexico

1862 Bismarck the Prussian Minister-President
1863 Schleswig-Holstein question re-emerged
1865 Death of Palmerston
1866 Austro-Prussian War
1867 North German Confederation
      Defeat and death of Emperor Maximilian in Mexico
1869 Opening of the Suez Canal
1870 Franco-Prussian War
      Surrender of Napoleon III at Sedan
      Overthrow of the Second Empire
      Third Republic established
      Annexation of the Papal States by Italy
      King Victor Emmanuel made Rome his capital.

Index

Aberdeen, Lord 101, 103
absolute monarchy 17
Act of Union (Ireland) 22
Alexander I, Tsar of Russia 28, 42–9, 74, 123
Alexander II, Tsar of Russia 59, 61–5, 123
American Revolution 12
Anglo-American relations 30–1
Arakcheev, Aleksei 47
Austerlitz, Battle of (1805) 44
Austro-Prussian War (1866) 82, 89–90, 95, 124

Baltic Theatre (1854–6) 105–6
Bastille, fall of 11, 13
Bismarck, Otto von 5–8, 10, 69, 87, 89, 94, 96–8, 109, 112
Blanc, Louis 37
Blanqui, Auguste 36
Bonaparte, Napoleon 6–7, 16–17, 23–4, 30, 36, 43–4, 74
Bourbon monarchy 5, 19, 25–7, 34–5
Burke, Edmund 14
Byron, Lord 75

Canning, George 22, 29–30, 76, 123
Capodistrias, Ioannis 74
Castlereagh, Viscount, Robert Stewart 22–33
Catholic Church 15–16, 35, 56, 82, 84
Cavaignac, General 54
Cavour, Count Camillo Benso, di 78–82, 84–6, 123
Charles Albert, King of Piedmont 56, 78
Charles X, King of France 37–8
Chartism, 52
Congress System 23, 27–8
Congress of Aix-la-Chapelle (1818) 29, 123

Congress of Vienna (1815) 22, 25, 27, 46, 48, 92
conservatism 14
Continental System 44, 46
Crimean War (1854–6) 99–108, 114
Crispi, Francesco 84–5

Declaration of the Rights of Man and the Citizen 11, 13, 19
Depretis, Agostino 84

Enlightenment, the 72–3
Erfurt Union, the 89
First Republic, France 18, 20
Four Ordinances of St Cloud (1830) 37
Four Points, the (1854) 102–3
Franco-Prussian War (1870–1) 82, 110, 112
Frankfurt, Treaty of (1871) 110
French Revolution (1789) 5–8, 11–21, 40, 72–3
French Revolution (1830) 35–40
French Revolution (1848) 35, 37–40, 53–4

Garibaldi, Giuseppe 57, 67, 81–2, 84–6, 121, 123
Gastein, Convention of 89
George III, King of England 17
German Confederation, the 88–9, 91
Giolitti, Giovanni 84
Graham, Sir James 101–2, 104–5
Greek revolt, the 32
Greek War of Independence 70–7, 123
Guizot, Francois 38, 52–3

Habsburg Empire 55–6, 67
Habsburg monarchy 28, 43, 53
Holy Alliance 28, 67, 75, 114

Il Risorgimento 78
industrialisation 8–10, 40

Jacobin Republic 15, 20
Jena, Battle of (1806) 44

Karlsbad Decrees (1819) 48, 123
Kleinstaaterei 93
Kolokotronis, Theodorus 75
Königgrätz, Battle of (1866) 90–1
Kulturkampf 97

laissez-faire 10, 51
Latin America, policy towards
30
Leipzig, Battle of (1813) 24, 94
liberalism 10, 27–8, 52, 67–9
Light Brigade, Charge of 100
Liverpool, Lord 23, 28
London, Treaty of (1827) 76
Londonderry, Marquis of 29
Louis Philippe, King of France
36, 39, 52–3, 123
Louis XVI, King of France 6, 13,
18
Louis XVIII, King of France 5,
26, 34, 37

Magenta, Battle of (1859) 119
Mahmud II, Sultan 74, 76
Malmo, Treaty of (1848) 54
Marx, Karl 13
Marseillaise, the 5, 21
Mazzini, Giuseppe 57, 81, 86,
121
Metternich, Prince Clemens 10,
14, 24–5, 28–9, 32, 48, 52–4,
109
Mill, John Stuart 8
millet system 71
Mirabeau, Compte de 6

Napoleon III, Louis Napoleon
19, 35, 53–4, 57, 90, 101,
103–4, 109–115
Napoleonic Ideas (1839) 35, 113

Napoleonic Wars (1799–1815) 7,
9, 68, 92–3
National Convention, France 13
National Liberal Party,
Germany 92, 97
nationalism 21, 28, 67–9, 70–77
Nationalverein (National
Association) 90–1, 93–4, 96
Navarino, Battle of (1827) 76,
123
Nicholas I, Tsar of Russia 101–2,
123
Nightingale, Florence 100
North German Confederation
90, 123

Olmutz, Convention of 89
Orleanist Dynasty 36–7
Orsini, Felice 110, 113
Ottoman Empire 32, 44, 70–7

Palmerston, Lord 22, 32, 102–3,
105
Paris Commune (1871) 50
Paris Peace Conference (1856)
107, 110
Paris, Treaty of (1814) 34
Paris, Treaty of (1815) 34
Pasha, Ali 73–4
Pétain, Marshal 5
Petrov, Anton 63, 65
Pitt, William 22–4, 32
Plombières, Compact of (1858)
110, 123
Polignac, Prince de 37, 39
primogeniture 6

Raglan, Lord 100
*Reflections on the Revolution in
France* 14
Reformverein (Reform
Association) 95–6
Revolutionary Land Settlement,
France 35
Revolutionary Wars, France
6–7, 9

Revolutions, European (1848) 50–8, 78–9
Russian Empire 40, 44

St Petersburg, Treaty of (1826) 76
sansculottes 20
Schleswig-Holstein 54–5, 89, 95–6, 124
Second Empire, France 109–10
Second Republic, France 53, 109–11, 123
secularism 15
Sedan 110
serfs, emancipation of (Russia) 43, 47, 59–66
Sevastopol, Siege of 99–100, 104–5
slave trade 27
Smith, Adam 10
socialism 20, 36–7, 67
Society of the Rights of Man 36
Solferino, Battle of (1859) 123
Speranskii, Mikhail 44–6

State Council, Russia 43, 45
States General, France 13

Third Estate, France 13
Third Republic, France 6, 18–19, 110–11
Tourkokratia 72
Trafalgar, Battle of (1805) 44

Unification of Germany 50, 58, 69, 87–98
Unification of Italy 50, 58, 69, 78–86

Vatican, the 81
Victor Emmanuel II, King of Italy 81, 123
Villafranca, Truce of 82, 110, 123
Voltaire, Francoise Marie Arouet 11

Waterloo, Battle of (1815) 25, 94, 123
Wellington, Duke of 23, 25, 29
William I, King of Prussia 89–90

Ypsilantis, Alexander 74–5